ICONIC WEALTH

C000043197

How to grow your incom

live a fulfilling life!

18 Women Share Their Wisdom

KYLIE ANDERSON

(Series 1)

MAPLE
PUBLISHERS

Iconic Wealth for Women (Series 1)

Author: Kylie Anderson

Copyright © Kylie Anderson (2023)

The right of Kylie Anderson to be identified as author of this work has been asserted by the author in accordance with section 77 and 78 of the Copyright, Designs and Patents Act 1988.

First Published in 2023

ISBN 978-1-915996-02-2 (Paperback)

Book cover design and Book layout by:
White Magic Studios
www.whitemagicstudios.co.uk

Published by:
Maple Publishers
Fairbourne Drive, Atterbury,
Milton Keynes,
MK10 9RG, UK
www.maplepublishers.com

"Being rich is having money;
Being wealthy is having time"

– Margaret Bonnano

Contents

.

Foreword

Penny Power OBE

Founder of "Business is Personal"

Believe that *"Business is Personal, and you can lead the life and business you want".*

As I write this foreword my desire is for this book to have an impact on your life. That is the driving force for Kylie, aware of the challenges that many women have to not only create a business that serves them while they serve others, but also build long term wealth.

In my 40 years in business, I have had some great successes and some painful challenges. I have learned that business is not straight forward, we need to constantly learn, adapt and connect with others. Aside from the work we do to serve clients, we are running in the background a complex life of supporting many people and progressing our skills in a world that places many obstacles and many opportunities.

My experience of learning business was very hands-on. I didn't learn it in school, university or take time out to do an MBA, I learned through the lessons I had to experience. I never felt I had time to study; ensuring I could pay my bills, manage the team around my business, build my brand and maintain the loving relations around me took all the time I had outside of client activities. I experienced loneliness in my social life, I experienced challenging investors, I experienced financial fear and yet, I was always driven by the impact and dreams I had for the business world to be a better place for women, and for those men that also found it hard.

The greatest asset I had was my lack of fear around being me. This was not as a result of a high ego, this was driven by the desire I had to have real conversations with other business people. I was never taken in by the 'wealth' displayed online, I had witnessed the fake way that people were choosing to build their brands and client base. I then often witnessed the crumbling impact of their truth and the lack of friends they had. It is so easy to hire a flash car for the day, rent a house for a week, buy a branded suit and then take it back. I was determined that I would find the people in life that had values far deeper than money and the display of money.

Kylie and her tribe share the realness of life in business and the need for women to focus on not only generating the income and life they desire, but to build longer term wealth as well. To embrace investing, to discover philanthropy and to create bigger visions to make a real impact! The tips and insights they provide will help the reader to create a balanced fulfilling life and business they love, along with sharing various wealth vehicles and new ideas they may not have even considered yet.

Kylie wants people to have freedom of choice and independence. Independence and freedom starts by being free to be the real you, to proudly share your real journey, to know that your vulnerabilities around money, wealth and areas of business that you need help with does not affect your credibility and the skills you have to help your clients.

Business, like any other wealth vehicle, is a journey of lifelong learning. It cannot be learned in the classroom. It's about taking action and making it happen. Enjoy this book and the insights and wisdom each writer is sharing, and congratulations to Kylie for the impact she has and continues to seek to have through knowing you as one of her readers.

**"If Good Women
Earn Good Money
They Do Good Things!"**

– Kylie Anderson

Introduction

Welcome to Iconic Wealth for Women,

Did you know that 1 in 5 women are going to be in poverty in the UK in retirement...?

And women invest 40% less than men!

These were some of the statistics that kicked my b**** to finally get it together and launch Iconic Wealth for Women in a much bigger way.

You see, I've been working at launching and scaling online businesses for the last 5 years now (plus 15 years corporate sales and business experience before that, doing millions of dollars' worth of deals). And one of the things I've always been frustrated by is watching incredible women, with amazing skills, struggling for money!

Whether that's because:

- They are not charging enough for their services.
- They don't understand how to manage their money and numbers.
- They don't have basic business skills, or
- Whether it's because they are held back by crippling mindset blocks and limiting beliefs.

And often avoid thinking about it altogether!

Maybe you can relate?

And the BIG thing is – **we often don't talk about wealth or money at all!**

And why shouldn't we? I love MONEY (yes, I said it) as it totally gives me freedom of choice – to spend time travelling, to help my family (and many others) and to make a difference.

There is a lot of "Ego" around money, especially in the online space – fast cars, exotic holidays, designer clothes, but look behind the scenes and the reality is nothing like the facade that is shown to the world.

Why – because to be open about money and wealth is quite scary!

It's often shunned upon too. If you do share your money success often you experience bullying (and yes unfortunately a lot from other women) or hear things like – you are just money driven, all you do is talk about money!

BUT most of us that make and talk about money – don't do it for the sake of money. I don't think I've met one successful female entrepreneur making incredible money that does it for money. **WE do it to create impact.** Whether that's in our own lives, our family lives or in society!

Yet often we are seen as being "money driven".

Well what does that even mean? And who cares if we really are! – the key thing is what you do with that money and who you impact. I've often been heard saying –

"If good women earn good money they do good things!"

And yep, that's right.

The women I know who make and create amazing money and build long term wealth, generally have an incredible impact on their family. They are often involved in social and philanthropic ventures as well. Changing society one step at a time.

That's why **Iconic Wealth for Women had to be launched – it's about women who unapologetically want it all and aren't scared to embrace having money conversations.**

I'm now on a mission to transform the lives of a million women around the globe to create financial freedom, independence and choice!

And it all starts with **COMMUNITY!**

So, no matter where you are on your wealth journey this book and community has something for you.

When looking at building your wealth there are many options you can choose from and a variety of vehicles that can help you get there – like building an online business, trading stocks/shares, investment and growing your property portfolio, building and acquiring businesses and so much more!

It can seem overwhelming and confusing, but you could start by asking yourself:

What skills and experience do I have?

What do you enjoy doing and are interested in?

What access to resources do I have (time, money etc)?

What is my vision, and goals I want to achieve?

Then once you've done a quick audit, you can start to look at what you might create, invest in or learn to build your long-term wealth.

The most important thing however is to GET STARTED!

It is never too late to start!

I've been lucky enough to meet and be surrounded by the most incredible women from around the globe (and you are going to meet some of them in this book) who have turned their lives around (even over the age of 40), with diverse backgrounds and experiences to build incredible wealth and the lifestyle they truly desire.

And if they can do it – so can YOU!

I hope this book will inspire you, motivate you and start to educate you to take action and be brave to build not only your income but your long-term wealth as well.

Because money is just a resource to change your own life and those around you too.

It gives you FREEDOM OF CHOICE!

Choice to help your family.

Choice to live the lifestyle you truly desire.

Choice to help others and create societal change!

It takes the pressure off, removes a lot of stress and makes life all that much brighter.

So are you ready?

In this book we have a line-up of incredible women who are going to share with you a little bit about their world of wealth, how they created it and more importantly how you can get started too.

Don't forget to JOIN the Iconic Wealth for Women Community:

www.iconicwealthforwomen.com

And get your Free Book Resources

www.iconicwealthforwomen.com/book-resources

And you'll gain all the support you need, connect with fabulous women and tap into some core resources to help you get started.

See you on the inside.

Your host, Kylie Anderson

Online Business Strategist & Award Winning Coach

The Origins of an African Proverb …

"If you want to go fast, go alone; but if you want to go far, go together."

CHAPTER 1

Do Your Finances Look Like Something Out of the MATRIX?

ABBY ANDERSON
Bookkeeper and Founder of Rock Solid Accounting

Do your finances look like something out of the MATRIX? Lots going on but you don't have a clue what the numbers mean or how to utilise them?

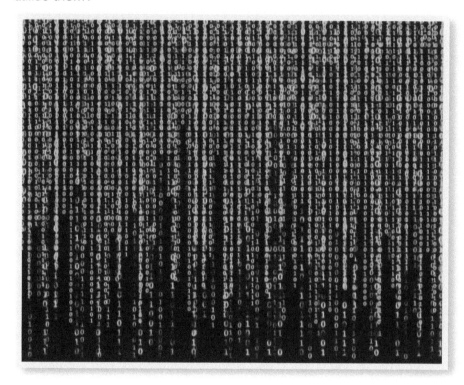

For those who know the film, The Matrix, you'll understand my analogies!

I challenge you to STOP taking the BLUE pill (stuck in a 'same shit, different day' reality) and start taking our RED pill (explore the bigger picture, whether that is outsourcing or to get a better understanding of the numbers yourself).

So, who am I?

Hi, I'm Misses Anderson (Abby). No, not Neo's wife but close enough to Trinity. I kick butt just as good! I currently run 2 business, Rock Solid Accounting UK Ltd is my Bookkeeping practise (of 10 years) and the other is the next level stuff of Unlocking Hidden Profit in your business, Trinity Finance Coaching.

I'm not what you call a 'typical' bookkeeper, as our profession has always had a slight stigma and so I'm guessing you might be thinking we are all boring?! I could be wrong, but I intend on changing your perspective on what I do, how I do it and show you I'm a human with a sense of humour. I have been a bookkeeper for almost 30 years (yes, that long!) and I have never fallen out of love with making a huge impact on my client's business & personal finances and lives!

I also love being creative.... not with bookkeeping I hasten to add, but you can find me doing my arty farty stuff in my spare time. I have a beautiful 19-year-old daughter, Aimee, who is more 'out out' than 'in in' and she's loving life in the big city of London, working for a Law Firm.... she didn't follow in her mother's footsteps! Whereas I did, and thanks to my Mum, Viv, when I was as little as 7 years old, I had a calculator in one hand and a ledger in the other (yes, it was pen and paper in those days).

So, I'm assuming you want to grow and scale your business, yes? Then you need to have a good understanding of your personal and business finances! Yes, I did mention personal finances here, as believe it or not, the relationship you have with your personal finances impacts your business finance functionality.

Personal Finance NOW

I mentor clients to firstly look at their personal finances by completing an analysis of their spend. I totally get it that this may seem scary. But trust me, it's revolutionary if you're a business owner – I want you to put your big, brave pants on and take these simple steps...you really won't regret it!

"If you don't get serious about your money you will never have serious money."
– Grant Cardone

Goals

Most goals come with a monetary value to them. I remember I wanted a hot tub for the garden. I had to research not only how much it cost, but the groundwork, fitting, electricity consumption and then the upkeep with chemicals etc too. I then put a date on when I wanted it installed. I really didn't want to put it on credit and so I calculated how much extra per month I needed from my business to hit this goal.

If you already have your goals set out or you have an idea what your goal is going to be, then write them here:

	WHAT / VISION	DATE	COST
6 MONTHS			
1 YEAR			
2 YEAR			
3 YEAR			
4 YEAR			
5 YEAR			
10 YEAR			

"A dream written down with a date is a goal. A goal broken down into steps, becomes a plan. A plan, backed up by action, makes your dreams come true."

– Greg Reid

Personal Finance FUTURE

Once I had worked out the extra cost to achieve my goal, I was then able to see what my FUTURE personal finances would be on a monthly basis.

"If your dreams don't scare you, they are too small."
– Richard Branson

Business Finance NOW

There are 12 Key Numbers in your business you should be monitoring weekly to have full clarity and control over the growth of your business:

1. Leads

There are many variations depending on what industry and business you're in.

This could be the number of visitors to your website or your trade show stall.

2. Conversion Rate (Leads to Prospects)

This is the rate you convert your Leads to Prospects shown as a percentage.

You may be asking, what is a good conversion rate?

Honestly? It depends on a number of areas.

When it comes to conversion rate, there's no one-size-fits-all approach.

Conversion rates vary by industry, marketing source, average sales length and more.

Low-ticket items are easier to sell whereas higher-value leads can be more difficult to convert and can generally require more time and assistance to decide whether or not they should make a purchase.

It also depends on what strategy you use at each conversion level.

For example:

A Lead to Prospect conversion could be a Lead Magnet on your socials where they entered their details to obtain an e-book or fact sheet. This is where Leads have shown an interest in your product/service and they then become a prospect.

If you're new to business and you're not sure what your conversion rate is, then carry out some research of your industry and find out what the consensus is for this conversion level.

3. Prospects

We defined what a prospect is, above. Prospects have to be nurtured, so ensure you have this area covered in your Sales CRM or funnel.

4. Conversion Rate (Prospects to Clients/Customers)

This is the rate you convert your Prospects to Customers. This number is extremely important as it will determine how many Leads you need.

A Prospect to Customer conversion could be where you've had a phone call or a Zoom meeting and you have signed them up during those conversations. If you're new to business and you're not sure what your conversion rate is, then carry out some research of your industry and find out what the consensus is for this conversion level.

5. Total New Clients/Customers or Number of Sales

This should be an easy number to obtain – the total number of Sales you've made or number of new clients/customers you've gained.

6. Average Order Value/Average Transaction Value

I understand that each client/customer might be paying a much higher price than others, but you still need to divide the total revenue by the total number sales to obtain an average order value i.e. £25,000 ÷ 20 = £1,250.

7. Total Revenue (Recurring & Ad-hoc)

This is the total Number of Sales multiplied by the Average Order Value.

8. Direct Costs

Direct costs are the purchases you make that are directly associated with the Sale of an item. For example, you had to buy widgets to make a product before you could sell it. Also, if you had a freelancer who put those widgets together to make the product, their costs would go here. However, if you employed someone (PAYE), then this cost goes in Salaries see point 11 below.

9. Gross Profit & Gross Profit Margin (%)

GP – This is the amount that comes halfway down the Profit & Loss statement. In the example above it is £25,000 – £5,000 = £20,000. This is the amount left over to fund your Overheads, Salaries & Profit. GP% – This is the Gross profit divided by the Total Revenue (multiplied by 100 to get the %).

10. Overheads

These are your fixed and variable expenses that your business pays to Suppliers to function. These are the costs you have to pay regardless of you selling anything! Don't include your salaries here, this comes next.

11. Salaries

These are your staff costs. Those that are on your PAYE. If you employ a sub-contractor (i.e. someone who is not on your Payroll) that:

i)   is needed to perform their services to enable a sale i.e. an engineer to build an engine to sell then this goes as part of your Direct Costs (Cost of Goods sold)

ii) is needed to perform services to enable the running of the business i.e. a Sales Manager is part of your Overheads

12. Net Profit

This is what is left after you've paid all your expenditure. This is what allows you to increase your earnings or re-invest into your business!

So, where is your business right NOW? Use the table below to define those numbers:

How many Leads are you getting every month?	
What is the Conversion Rate?	
How many Prospects are you getting every month?	
What is the Conversion Rate?	
How many Sales are you making every month?	
What is the number of Sales you made?	
What is your AOV/ATV	
What is your Recurring Income?	
What is your Ad-hoc Income?	
What are your Direct Costs?	
What is your Gross Profit & Gross Profit Margin?	
What Overheads do you currently have?	
What are your current Salaries/Staff costs?	
What is your Net Profit?	

To download a copy of the template, which includes a personal finance analysis, goals, business finance analysis and the tweaks calculator, go to:

https://linktr.ee/unlockhiddenprofit it costs £47 (special price if you use this discount code UHPWKSHT22)

"Know your Numbers, Change your Life."

– Abby Anderson

Unlocking the HIDDEN profits

Now we get to the juicy part (and the part that I absolutely love). If you've ACTUALLY completed the above and you've made it here, I am getting very excited for you.....yes, I probably need to get a life!

Below is an example of a Business's current position and the small tweaks you could be making in your business, to uplift your Net Profit. By increasing the leads by 5% and reducing the salaries by 5%, the example below shows a £16.5K uplift!

Where are you NOW...

	Top down, current status	P/mth Now		Small Changes / Tweaks % change	
1	Leads	150		5%	158
	times				
2	Prospect Conversion	35%		5%	40%
	equals				
3	Prospects	53			63
	times				
4	Customer Conversion	35%		0%	35%
	equals				
5	No of New Sales	19			23
	times				
6	Average Order Value	£750	INCREASE	0%	£750
	equals				
7	Total New Revenue	£14,250			£17,250
	add				
	Current retained Client Revenue	6,000			6,000
	add				
	Adhoc Client Revenue	2,000			2,000
	equals				
	Total Revenue	22,250			25,250
	times				
8	Gross Margin %	50%		0%	50%
	equals				
9	Gross Profit	£11,125			£12,625
	minus				
10	Overheads	£1,237	DECREASE	0%	£1,237
	minus				
11	Salaries	£2,337		-5%	£2,454
	equals				
12	Net Profit *(before tax)*	£7,551			£8,934
	% Uplift in Net Profit				18%
	Uplift in 12 mths[+]				£16,598

If you decide you want to work backwards, where you know the extra net profit your business needs, below is an example of what tweaks are required. Based on the previous examples numbers and you needed a target net profit of £10K, then you would need a 43% in Leads and a 5% decrease in salaries to meet that target net profit.

Where you WANT TO BE...

Bottom Up, current & future status			
Tells you how many leads you need to achieve your target profit			
	Now	After	
No of Leads Needed	150	215	43%
Equals			
Prospect Conversion	35%	35%	0%
Divided by			
Prospects	53	75	
Equals			
Customer Conversion	35%	35%	0%
Divided by			
No of Sales	19	26	
equals			
Average Order Value	£750	£750	0%
Divided by			
Total New Revenue	£14,250	£19,382	
Equals			
Current retained Client Revenue	6,000	£6,000	
minus			
Adhoc Client Revenue	2,000	£2,000	
minus			
Total Revenue	£22,250	£27,382	
Divided by			
Gross Margin %	50%	50%	0%
Divided by			
Gross Profit	£11,125	£13,691	
Equals			
Overheads	£1,237	£1,237	0%
Plus			
Salaries	£2,337	£2,454	5%
Plus			
Target Net Profit *(before tax)*	£7,551	£10,000	

To download a copy of the **Excel template**, which includes a personal finance analysis, goals, business finance analysis and the tweaks calculator, go to: http://www.linktr.ee/unlockhiddenprofit and click the **Worksheets**- it costs £47 (special price if you use this discount code UHPWKSHT22)

If you'd prefer to just use a FREE template (you'd have to work the calculations out yourself), then you can download the **Know Your Numbers – e-workbook**.

Go to: http://www.linktr.ee/unlockhiddenprofit and click the e-workbook

"There will never be a right time. Stop waiting and start doing."
– Mel Robbins

Business Finance FUTURE

As you see from the previous examples, there are many different tweaks you could make to grow and scale your business from where it is now to where you want it to be.

Focus on 1-2 tweaks at a time. Build consistency and then move on to one of the others.

What tweaks will you make to UNLOCK SOME HIDDEN profit?

If you think you're too small to make an impact, try sleeping with a Mosquito!

FIND ME – ClubHouse (@abby-bookkeeper), LinkedIn (abby-anderson-rocksolid), Email: info@unlockhiddenprofit.com, Instagram (abby.rocksolid), Facebook (Trinity Finance Coaching & Know Your Numbers for Growth)

OTHER RESOURCES: https://linktr.ee/unlockhiddenprofit

"If you think you're too small to make a difference, try sleeping with a Mosquito!"
Dalai Lama

CHAPTER 2

**Even a Waitress Can Buy a Business
(And You Can Too!)**

DELLA KIRKMAN
Certified Public Accountant (CPA)

Once upon a time, in a faraway land called Indiana, there was a single mom waiting tables at a place called Cracker Barrel. One day, a little fairy whispered in her ear, "You should become a CPA." And so she did. Then she bought a CPA firm, later bought out her partner, and eventually sold the firm altogether.

It wasn't an easy path, and I did have help from a few fairy godmothers along the way, but in less than 10 years, my life did a complete 180. I went from daily money struggles and disconnect notices, to building a brand new home, having a fat bank account and financial freedom.

Not long before this adventure started, I was dumping my change jar on the floor of the car, searching for enough money to buy a couple days' worth of fuel. Oh, and the quarters were long gone, so it was dimes and nickels I was in search of. I often paid my bills in the order that things were scheduled to be shut off. It wasn't always that bad. My girls had music lessons, attended private school, and had plenty to eat. But it was a balancing act, and I often went without so they didn't have to.

We were getting by and waiting tables was great for our situation. I made cash every shift, could pick up extra work when needed, or give away a shift when there was a field trip or an upset tummy. I dropped them off and picked them up from school every day. I was room parent and Girl Scout leader, and I made dinner every night. That was why I became a mom in the first place.

As my youngest daughter began to transition to all day kindergarten, I felt it was time. Time to shift the focus back to me a bit. I wanted to use my degree, make some real money, and find a way into entrepreneurship that didn't put our already fragile lifestyle at risk. **I didn't have any money to buy a business, my first false notion**, and I couldn't go more than a couple of days without running the "savings account" dry.

I started with the help wanted ads. All the cool jobs I saw required either an MBA, which I didn't have, or a CPA. More naivete on my part. I thought, "Oh, a CPA. I'm a good test taker. I'll just take a test and become a CPA." You're probably smarter than I was, but I soon discovered that THE CPA Exam is actually four exams. They must all be passed within 18 months of each other. They're each 2-5 hours long. And they're hard.

The next blow came when I found out that even my double major in finance and economics didn't give me enough credits to even be eligible to take the exams. I was short on total credits and short on accounting credits.

Back to campus I went. It took me two semesters and a summer session in between to get "caught up". In the meantime, I found a tiny tax firm that was willing to hire me. I had no experience doing taxes, except for the few returns I had completed for my brother's friends, uhhh, in exchange for alcohol. I left that off my resume. This firm was willing to hire me to do drop-offs. That's where you sit in a room in the back and do data entry, make a list of missing items and questions. No customer interaction. No pressure. Someone else that knew what they were doing would check and correct all my work. On my very first day, the owner, an older gentleman who was also the main preparer, fell on the ice, shattered his hip into a million pieces (on top of all his other health issues) and never came back that entire tax season. To say it was a shit show is putting it mildly. I stuck it out, took on way more responsibility, and together, our small team made it through tax season, and saved Ralph's practice. When he returned to the office that spring, **I let him know I was interested in buying his business if he ever wanted to sell. I had no idea how I would make it happen, but I put that little nugget out to the universe.**

I continued to work at the firm AND at the restaurant. I finished my extra courses, then passed all four CPA exams on the first try, within six months of each other! A pretty rare feat, even if I do say so myself. Ralph and I talked about me taking over his practice, but I was still so inexperienced. He also entertained an offer from a much larger regional firm, but he didn't think they would be a good fit for his small-town clients. **A seller motivated by something more than cash.**

Ralph's setup was a little unique. There were two separate firms operating in the same space, sharing overhead items like paper, printers, postage, utilities and rent. They did not share clients. They operated very independently from each other. I worked for the old guy, Ralph. Doug was a younger guy, but still a little older than me. Ralph had had an established practice for many years. At some point, Doug asked if he could use some of Ralph's office space to go out on his own. That relationship started long before I came around, but since

Ralph was there first, he controlled the space, the phone number, and the fax line, if you remember those.

As Ralph got more serious about selling, I'm sure Doug became more and more nervous. Ralph's sale would inevitably have a big impact on Doug's business; someone else would control the lease, the phone number and so on. Doug thought about buying Ralph's practice, the one that I worked for, but he didn't really want a second practice. **A buyer motivated by something other than cash.** He did want control. So much so, that he approached me with the idea of him buying Ralph's practice, and me managing it for him as an employee. I told him I wanted to be an owner, not an employee. **Putting it out to the Universe again.** I was upfront with him. I told him I didn't have any money for a down payment and I didn't think I could get a loan at that point. **I did have time. I wanted to work and learn, and I was good with the clients, an accountant with a personality!** Unbelievably, Doug came back and offered me 49% equity in exchange for running the practice and handling the day-to-day tasks! **A partner motivated by more than money.**

We made it official at the tail end of 2011, right before my 40th birthday. Whew! That was a close call. I was finally going to "be somebody". As I said, Doug didn't really want another business, so we continued to keep the two firms very separate. Doug ran his original business, and I ran the new business, the one that used to belong to Ralph.

Here is how the deal went down:
- For $0 out of my pocket, I received 49% equity.
- Doug paid Ralph $10,000 upfront for the office equipment and supplies.
- The purchase of the business itself consisted of monthly payments over five years, based on revenue generated from the acquired clients. The business paid for itself. No loan.
- Ralph stayed on as a part-time W-2 employee.
- I ran the entire practice-with lots of guidance from Doug, and Ralph for that matter.

- I received a small salary which covered all my living expenses. Way more than I was making at the Barrel!
- Plus, I received a bonus at year end, based on new clients I brought in.
- Every December, we emptied the bank account, except for about $15,000 to cover the next year's beginning working capital.
- We split that distribution based on our 51/49 ownership percentages.

I was in heaven! I finally had some control of my own destiny! And I'm just going to shout this out, I still love taxes!

Due to Ralph's health issues mentioned above, his practice had been struggling. Revenues were declining and missed deadlines meant clients were going elsewhere. I won't go into all the details, but this was a turnaround situation. When Doug and I took over, we generally kept everything the same. Clients may not have even noticed the change in ownership unless they read the name on the door. Yes, my name was on the door! We enhanced customer service with items such as a website, an e-newsletter, a secure portal, texting capabilities and digital storage instead of paper. We never missed a deadline. I ran the firm and did all the client interaction, along with my staff. Doug was instrumental, but very much behind the scenes, just the way he liked it. He was still running his own separate firm, plus, he was reviewing all our business returns. It was a winning combination! There were certainly challenges to overcome, but business was great and growing.

Then, out of the blue, early in the tax season of 2015, Doug announced that he wasn't checking our business returns any more. We were on our own. Progress, right? Then I thought, "if he's not helping us anymore, I may as well buy him out and run this show on my own." And that's exactly what I did!

The partner buyout deal went like this:

- This was the fourth year of the original purchase, so most of the profits were going to pay Ralph off.
- Doug and I were 51/49 shareholders in an S corporation.

- He wanted his 51% of the retained earnings as his buyout price.
  - This was money he had been taxed on, but never put in his pocket.
  - I offered to pay that amount in two payments, one at the end of 2015 and one at the end of 2016.
- These two years I was paying both gentlemen.
- But it all came out of company profits!
- Never out of my pocket or through debt.

I did not put much money in my savings over those 5 years, but I did end up with a money-making asset, free and clear.

For the next year and a half, Doug and I continued on much as we had been, sharing space and utilities and such. We were both growing and expanding, and he wanted to bring his son-in-law into his practice. We searched for a new office big enough to accommodate both of our businesses together, to no avail. Then in the summer of 2016, Doug ended up finding an office space for just his business and he moved out of our shared space. It was a little rough, a bit unexpected, but it turned out to be a blessing in disguise.

My business continued to grow. We implemented more technologies, increased our prices, and focused on community and customer service. As the sole owner with no debt on the business, I was finally able to start creating wealth. And things were good. Hell, they were great! I bought a motorcycle, paid off my truck, and built a new house, all while growing my bank account, too. But over time, the shine began to wear off. With all the pandemic regulations, tax laws changing every day, it just wasn't fun anymore. I'm a big believer in fun. Not that every task must be filled with giggles and smiles, but one should truly enjoy their daily work. I was no longer enjoying this business, and it was time, once again, to make a change.

In June of 2020, I decided to sell, or at least try to sell my practice. I wasn't sure what to expect. If it didn't sell, oh well. The money was still coming in. I would find a way to pivot and make it work. If it did sell, I could move on to something else. I always considered the firm as a stepping stone, a stepping stone to... I don't know exactly, something bigger and better, something with a broader reach.

I feel like the luckiest girl in the world, but I know it's not just luck. I show up. I say 'yes' as often as possible, even when I'm scared. And I'm willing to risk looking foolish if I have a chance to try something new, a chance to reach for the next rung. And luck struck again because my practice sold within 3-4 months. I received 90% of the funds upfront with an earnout on just the remaining 10%. I was 48 years old at the time of the sale. I got a late start, but it all worked out.

Now I have the time and financial freedom to pursue only the fun projects. I'm preparing my young adult daughter to buy a duplex for house hacking and we're in hot pursuit of a business for her to buy. By the time she's 40, she'll be leaps and bounds beyond me. And that's the joy of parenthood, of mentorship, and of entrepreneurship.

If being a business owner is in your heart, but not yet in your life, I highly recommend the following steps to get started on the path to Acquisition Entrepreneurship:

1. Make your intentions known to the Universe, even if you're unsure of how to make the thing happen. Would you like to own the company you work for? Mention it to your boss. Are you dreaming of owning a coffee shop? Tell your Barista you would love to have a place like that one day. You never know who may be listening, and YOU may be exactly what they need.

2. Understand that business sellers, business buyers, and business partners often have motivations beyond money. In a study of business sellers, it was revealed that 68% of them were motivated to sell by something other than money. The most common reason cited was having a safe pair of hands to continue to grow and care for their business "baby".

3. Think of a business as an asset that can be bought, improved upon and sold, just like any other asset, just like real estate, for example. A business doesn't have to be a lifelong commitment. Entrepreneurs get restless and are fascinated by the next shiny opportunity. Make this a part of your strategy if that works for you.

4. Have fun with entrepreneurship and enjoy the adventure.

Peace out!

Della is the publisher of the Shift-N-Gears.com bi-weekly newsletter, designed to help people buy, grow and sell small businesses. The free newsletter is part of a larger, developing educational platform for encouraging women to pursue their dreams of entrepreneurship through acquisition, buying a profitable business that can support their lifestyle, rather than the hard, risky path of the start-up.

CHAPTER 3

Six Steps to Invest

EMMA WRIGHT
APFS Chartered Financial Planner

"The UK now boasts 2,000 ISA millionaires – and the top 60 have pots averaging a whopping **£6.2million**, official data has revealed for the first time."

Source: https://investingreviews.co.uk/blog/uk-has-2000-isa-millionaires/

It is easy to become an ISA millionaire, every woman can achieve this goal with a little time, commitment, money and know-how.

All you need to do is take six simple steps, consistently and persistently, over **time**.

Time is your biggest asset.

Just imagine if you invested £500 a month into a diversified global portfolio of stocks for 30 years, reinvesting your average investment returns each year, you would likely be the owner of an investment portfolio worth £1mn.*

* (This example is based on an investment generating 10% per annum annually compounded. This is purely for demonstrational purposes to highlight the power of compounding your investment returns over time.)

The compound impact of simply getting started and making the most of every £1 you make is epic.

Who am I to talk to you about investing?

I am **just** a girl from Bradford after all. A northern city in the UK that doesn't honestly inspire wealth. Through my love of mathematics and sheer determination, I graduated from The University of Manchester with a first class in Financial Accounting and Derivatives, enabling myself to get a top job in the City of London at US investment banking giant, Citigroup. My drive for **independence** and the belief you have to work hard to get what you want from life, is how I landed my dream job on the dealing floor of RBS Markets where I spent almost a decade trading investments and navigating the ups and downs of financial markets.

What's crazy is, it was only when I decided to leave the big smoke, in pursuit of a better life in North Devon, when I became a Chartered Financial Planner, that I realised how much time, energy and money I wasted during my time in London. Despite working with investments, I did not appreciate the impact of doing my own. Nor did I realise just how much money I was leaking to unnecessary tax. Although I understood the stock market, I didn't know the importance of financial planning and utilising my annual tax allowances.

I left London because I wanted a better life. If only I had known how to start my own investments during my time in London, to leverage the money I was making and create more wealth for myself. Nobody told me how to hold on to my money, it was all about earning a big salary and spending it on a very nice lifestyle.

I would likely be in a far stronger financial position right now had I had a financial planner by my side.

In recent years, since I started my little family, I had an awakening that I needed to do more. Although I loved financial planning, I had this urge that I wasn't having the impact I wanted and I had a burning desire, with a climate crisis on our hands, to do my part to help save our amazing planet. Without a planet there is no wealth. So, I launched my own financial planning and wealth management coaching business to enable me to have the impact I wanted to have around the world. My personal mission is to help reverse the impact of the global climate crisis, restoring the global biosphere, £1 sustainable investment at a time.

I firmly believe that if more wealth builds in the hands of those who want to have a positive impact, the greater that positive impact will be. It is a ripple effect. Especially if more female entrepreneurs' step into the wealth they deserve by being empowered to start investing.

What's holding you back from investing?

Often, as women, we believe that we have to work harder to make money. We are constantly told about the gender pay gap. I think hard work pays dividends, mind the pun. What doesn't serve us as women is how we often waste our most valuable asset, time, by not valuing ourselves and our contribution, and we end up not holding on to enough of the money we make by giving it away somehow, and there we don't feel we have enough surplus income to warrant starting an investment.

What stops women from investing is fear. It can be the fear of losing our hard-earned money because we think investing is risky. By being risk averse and believing it is safer to hoard our money in cash, we end up over saving and missing out. The fear of the unknown, because we simply don't understand how to get started.

And simply believing that we can't possibly be an investor, this is a big **blocker**.

Fundamentally, historically as women, we are not the hunter gathering risk takers. We are conditioned by nature to believe it is our responsibility to be the carers, which leads to habits like over-giving, overspending and focussing on everyone else's needs ahead of our own. Which means we perceive investing as being a selfish act, it is putting our future needs ahead of looking after others in the present moment.

However, by starting your own investment journey you are building your financial resilience, your independence, which makes you stronger, even for those around you. You are building your financial security and freedom. Investing part of your income, over time, is how you build wealth. It is actually quite a boring and very simple process, when you know how.

And it is definitely not selfish, it is essential to your survival and independence over time.

By becoming an investor, even with just £1, you're sending a very clear message to your subconscious that you can do this and you are worthy.

Investing is how the rich get richer. It is what enables you to be able to retire one day, when you own enough assets that pay for your lifestyle, without needing to go to work. It is how you create, grow and protect your wealth from hidden risks, like the rising cost of living, aka inflation.

By the end of this chapter, you will not only feel motivated and empowered to get started, you will feel excited and want to take that vital next step of hitting invest.

Six Steps To Invest

As a Chartered Financial Planner, and ex investment banker, I left giving regulated financial advice to found my financial coaching, planning and educational business, Independent Wealth, to focus on what matters.

Financial Planning

"Vanguard found that clients with a financial planner benefited on average by around 3% per annum more than those without."

The power of building and managing wealth isn't in the products you buy; it is in financial planning.

This is the reason I launched my signature investment programme, Six Steps To Invest, to share the exact financial planning framework that I use with my 1-2-1 clients.

Your Six Steps To Invest:
- Step 1: Set your financial intention.
- Step 2: Select your investment.
- Step 3: Define on your personal attitude to investing.
- Step 4: Style your investment.
- Step 5: Select a platform or provider.
- Step 6: Hit invest!

Let's break it down:

Step 1: Set your financial intention

If you aren't clear on why you're investing, you will likely make mistakes. Give every £1 you make, a purpose; ask yourself what your investment is for. What is the time frame you have, when will you need access, investing for an income or for growth? Do you seek freedom before "retirement", independence when you choose, or are you investing for someone else like your children?

Be clear on what you want from your investment so that you can confidently take the next step.

Step 2: Select your investment account

Once you have your financial intention you can confidently select the most suitable investment account that will serve your needs.

Whether you live around the world, researching the types of investment accounts available so you can access the best tax reliefs and make the most of your investment returns, is an invaluable way to boost the performance of your investment over time.

I teach UK based investors on how they can select the right UK based investment accounts, such as whether to use an ISA or a pension. If you are investing for the longer term, you get vital tax reliefs and incentives from utilising a pension or a lifetime ISA. But if you seek financial freedom before retirement age, and need access before, then these types of accounts might not be suitable for your intention.

Step 3: Define on your personal attitude to investing

If you have £100 to invest, for 10 years, you will have saved £12,000. But what if you need or want £15,000?

In order to achieve the returns you seek, and ensure that your investment works as hard as it can for you over time, you need to be prepared to take some risk. But it is important to understand how risk vs returns works, and the risk of not taking enough risk.

When you invest in the stock market, day to day the price of shares moves up and down. These daily fluctuations are known as volatility, and it is this price volatility of assets that is the general measure of investment risk.

You're unlikely going to invest into a single share or investment. Typically when you get started you will invest via a large collective investment, known as a fund. A fund helps to mitigate investment risk in a number of ways, by being expertly managed and giving your potential access to a globally diverse universe of investments. Plus, it is very easy for you to select the risk you wish to take.

Funds that are regulated in the UK, and listed on platforms for you to access, clearly state their risk rating, which is on a scale of 1 and 7, 1 being very low risk and 7 being very high risk. This risk rating is determined by how volatile the fund is day to day. The more up the risk scale you move, the greater your expected return. Likewise, if you don't take enough risk then your investment over time could seriously under perform.

Time is an essential way of managing the risk you take. If you can leave your investment to grow, over time the fluctuations flatten and your investment has the opportunity it needs to grow.

Step 4: Style your investment

Styling your investment is essential for moulding it around your financial intention and your personal values. There are no square pegs into a round hole when you invest, you get to choose. Are you wanting to invest directly or indirectly via a fund, for growth or for income, passively or actively to generate outperformance?

And do you want to invest with impact, into ethical investments? There is so much you can do as an investor to have an impact with your wealth on the planet. When you invest, it is important to remember that you are giving a part of your money to a company in return for a share in its performance. You get to choose the companies you support, and how you want to invest.

Investing can do a huge amount of good, and collectively this is how we can create a ripple effect.

Step 5: Select a platform or provider

Once you have steps 1-4 nailed, you can confidently make an informed decision on where to set up your investment. Not all platforms or fund supermarkets are made equal. But you can discount and select a platform or provider, just like you would a bank account, when you are clear on what it is you want and need.

Step 6: Hit invest!

Just get started, and don't overthink it. You can't really go wrong when you are dripping money over time, a phenomenon known as pound-cost averaging. If you just want to get started then picking a general investment account is your safest bet, and just picking a global multi asset fund will likely serve your needs well.

It is better to invest, and be in the market, than being on the sidelines missing out, if you don't need that spare £1 in your bank account.

What's great is, you can use this framework for all of your investment pots, so every time you have a new intention, just follow the steps and you will be able to get started. In all honesty, you'll find starting an investment is just like opening a bank account when you realise how accessible and simple it is.

Do this one thing!

If you just want to get started, set up a Vegas fund.

Now this isn't as risky as it sounds. This is what I did when I lived in London and wanted to make the most of my spare £25 a month. I opened a general investment account with Hargreaves Lansdown, and I just selected a global fund from their Wealth Shortlist, and I hit invest.

If my investment made money, which it usually did, each year when I booked my girls' holiday I would sell the value of my investment, so the capital I had saved plus any profit I'd made paid for an even better holiday. Like upgrading my travel or my accommodation or having more spending money to do more nice things.

Not only did I save £25 I would have likely spent, I didn't fear losing it, so I didn't worry about making mistakes. But I learned how to use an investment platform, how to buy and sell, and my confidence grew.

Investing doesn't mean you can't access your money and enjoy it in the present moment. It is a common myth that investing in stocks is locking your money away. We are told that investing is for the long term due to the volatility in the short term, and if you pick an investment account that restricts your access. However, you can set up an investment that gives you income and access when you want it. You get to choose. Which is why starting with a general investment account can be super empowering.

My wealthy tip for you

Be clear on your vision, on your intention for your wealth.

You need to know why you're investing so you can correctly set up your investment but also feel connected to it and keep it up.

Create a vision board to support your investment. I use Pinterest and I create boards that represent all aspects of what I am building in my business and in my life.

The power of wealth building is to be consistent and persistent in the pursuit of it. The act of building wealth can be boring and simple, but it is what you do with that wealth that will have an impact on your life and leave a legacy worth remembering.

To connect with me and gain some valuable resources go to this link – https://myindependentwealth.com/wealth-resources/

CHAPTER 4

Role Models and Responsibilities

KIM UZZELL
Finance Coach & Mentor

Like many women of around my age (that's 52), in fact women of ANY age, I've gone through my adult life with that confusing mixture of wanting to break the mould, smash glass ceilings, be independent, "have it all", and yet at the same time, being held back in terms of my career, business, and financial success.

At times that has felt like two steps forwards and one step back. More often, though, it was one step forward, and two back.

I've pushed through, sort of. At times making progress and feeling like a trailblazer for women everywhere, and at other times accepting that this was, in some way, my lot….often giving up what I had successfully created before it really *did* get successful.

It's only relatively recently that I started to really work through the reasons for this yo-yo ing approach to my career and business. As I realised that I am entering what some would term my "third age", I did have that realisation that, having hit the fabulous age of 50 (yes, I was always determined to be fab at 50) it really was about time that I got this nut cracked. It was time to decide what I truly want to achieve for however many decades I have left, and then to work out a way of actually getting it without the same old things cropping up that have, for some reason, held me back before.

I'm not doing this just for me, but for my daughter, now 28, her children when she has them, and those generations that follow.

We have amazing futures ahead of us, but understanding our past will allow us to get the absolute best out of those futures.

I've spent over 30 years working with people and their money.

I've been a Tax lawyer, a Stockbroker, a Chartered Wealth Manager, and a Vice President for one of the biggest banks in the world.

But still I feel as though the surface, as far as women and their financial and career potentials are concerned, has barely been scratched.

Women have been on the "back foot" in terms of money for hundreds of years.

You don't have to look back too far to see women expected to stay home after starting a family, with the responsibility of earning the money going to the man of the house. Certainly, when I had my children in the mid 90's, it was the norm for women to take an extended career break, perhaps returning to a part time role when the youngest started school.

This might be no surprise – you may well have taken that break yourself, or had a circle of "stay at home" mum-friends. You might have had a mum who stayed at home while you and any siblings were very young. It's nothing unusual and, with maternity leave now being around 12 months, it is still considered by many to be the norm – that women stay at home when they start a family.

Go back just a few years and it was commonplace for girls and women not to be treated equally in an inheritance – the bulk of money, and any land/farming would have bypassed female offspring, and been inherited by the male "heir to the estate". The females would have received a smaller legacy or been provided with a dowry to take into their marriage. If two boys were born into a family, the term "an heir and a spare" were used. Was the same said of their sisters?

In some cultures, these "outdated" traditions are still considered to be standard practice – with women expected to be the home-maker, and not taking over the family interests in any business. We still see business signs showing ".....& Sons", although thankfully change is happening.

Perhaps more surprising, is that it wasn't until the 1960s that a woman could open her own bank account, and not until 1974 that the Equal Credit Opportunity Act was passed in the UK. Before that, lenders – banks and building societies – required women to have a male co-signer on any loan!

Could you imagine if we had to have our husband's, father's, or brother's signature not just on any credit card, loan, or mortgage application, but on every car lease arrangement, or even our mobile phone contracts – all of which are covered by the Consumer Credit legislation of the same year! Perish the thought!!

So why am I writing about these financial practices – which are becoming accepted as outdated now, as part of my own, and I suspect many others', journey of self-sabotage?

Two main reasons – both of which have a significant impact on the choices that we as women, whether in business or not, have today –

The first is to identify and address the resultant gaps that we have been experiencing in respect of levels of wealth and investment between men and women. We are slowly addressing the gender pay gap, but the issues and impacts go much deeper than that. Until we truly enable and encourage financial equality, in careers and business, this will not change.

The second is to understand the money mindset that we have inherited and taken with us throughout our own life – and which we may well be passing on to the next generation, whether we like it or not, whether we realise it or not.

I was brought up in an era where women were expected to stay at home – when a couple started a family, the Dad would go out to work and provide, and the Mum would keep house, raise the children, and perhaps return to work part time once the youngest reached school age, but may well not ever have returned to work other than perhaps the odd bit of selling Avon, Tupperware or Pippa-Dee (yes, I was a child of the 1970s!)

I am also a woman who chose a career in finance – more specifically in Stockbroking, a traditionally male dominated arena where until quite recently you were likely to get a job based on who your father was, which Public School you went to, and which golf course or shooting connections your family had. (I personally ticked NONE of those boxes!)

I know I generalise – but only to a point. Whilst the other professions of Law, Accountancy and the like moved quickly through the first part of the 21st century towards a better balance between genders, stockbroking was much slower to make that change. That part of the financial services industry, not just in the UK but across the Globe can at best be described as "work in progress". I left the Investment Management side of the industry after around 30 years, and over that time, saw the changes happening frustratingly slowly.

I had such high hopes though – for change to be rapid. For me to make my mark as some kind of trailblazer. Encouraging the industry to welcome the talented women out there, and encouraging those talented women to put themselves forward.

Because, although I had a modest, fairly typical upbringing for my generation, I come from a line of women who, on a career level (if not from an access to financial independence level) had bucked the expected generational trends.

My maternal grandmother, Mary, and my paternal grandmother, Kath, were both born in the early 1920s. Opposite ends of the country, but with similar working class backgrounds.

My Grandma was one of 9 children, born and raised in Lancashire, in the industrial north of England.

When many were leaving school at 14 and 15, Mary continued her education, with a desire to be a teacher. Not unusual on its own, but Mary chose maths to be her subject.

Further and higher education followed with a certificate in our family possession for "Advanced Mathematics and Needlework". I'm pretty sure none of the males of her cohort had to get a needle and thread out during class...

During the War, Mary and her pupils were evacuated from the targeted industrial North to the relative safety of rural East Anglia, where she met and married my Grandfather – a Norfolk farmer. Three children followed and one might have expected her to become a typical 1950's farmer's wife and full-time mum. Pinny on, bread baking, gathering eggs from the Chooks – very "Darling Buds of May".

Far from it.

My Grandma chose to continue teaching – not just a little bit here and there, but becoming headteacher of a local Comprehensive school – a challenge if ever there was one!

It was certainly not the path you would have expected her to take. But in doing so she set a career standard for those of us that followed!

But she was not the only one – Kath, my paternal grandmother was born and raised close to London. Excelling in administration and secretarial skills, she was working for a large insurance broker in London during the early part of the war, when she was approached and encouraged to join the Wrens....as part of the now legendary code breaking team based at Bletchley Park.

Of course, many women excelled in areas that they wouldn't have even been aware of if war hadn't broken out. Most, however, returned to more traditional family life in peacetime. Kath didn't.

My Nana met and married my Grandfather, Harry, and they went on to have 4 children. Harry was also very typical of the Cockney working class of the time.

Less "Darling Buds of May" and more "Call the Midwife" due to the London location, but again one would be wrong to assume her lot was set. Nana had other ideas.

Kath always wanted the best she could provide for her family. During the post-war years, with a toddler and a baby she invested in her career, and therefore in improving the future of her family.

In 1953, she paid 30 guineas (the equivalent of just over £3000 in today's money) to train as a surgical appliance fitter and receive her demonstration kit.

£3000 is a lot of money now. It would have felt even more then, when rationing was only just coming to an end, and the ability to just "pop it on a credit card", was a long way from being a possibility.

Nana put trust in herself, and had a belief that improvement was always available. That there was nothing out there to stop her, and her family, improving their chances in life.

The next two children came along and Kath continued to strive for improvement.

Moving out of London and up to Norfolk, she continued to work, and her P60s that she saved each year show a steady increase in her salary as she progressed in her administration career, at British Sugar and Campbells factories.

More than that, though, was her desire to keep learning.

Nana began her degree with the Open University in 1967.

She completed it some 20 years later.

Remember that this was decades before being able to catch up on replays of classes online. Sessions were held in the middle of the night on the BBC, or on radio. Alongside a family of 4, a career, her work with the Church, and the hundred and one committees that she was involved in, Nana made time to study.

Most of us would have given up.

She didn't.

And it wasn't enough, once she'd got her degree, she continued learning, well into her 80s, with certificates in various languages and IT skills taking their place in her certificate folder!

I was blessed with powerful female role models – who showed me that anything was possible, and that the expectation of society did not need to determine the career path that you could choose to take.

Two amazing role models. I've been left with big shoes to fill.

Alongside my financial career, I have continued with the coaching and mentoring string to my bow that I began in 2005 after suddenly losing my Dad, when I was looking for some magic form of self-healing.

Over time, this has developed into more specialist financial coaching, with a focus predominantly on women and a mission to give them the confidence to take control of their finances, and create and build their own wealth by earning more building through entrepreneurship, and by investing for their future financial choices.

Shockingly, at the time of writing this, women have around 40% less in their retirement pot than men. How can that be right?

This means that as we approach that point in life where we want to be doing our own thing, perhaps taking a step back from our corporate careers, perhaps getting out there and travelling the world in a way that we couldn't do while we were looking after our families, we continue to be on the back foot. And it has to change.

It is up to us, as women who have seen the greatest level of change in so many areas during our lifestyle – equality progress, acceptance of diverse cultures, introduction of technology (there WAS a life before the internet and mobile phones!), to take everything we have learned and to make sure that we pass on our experiences and our knowledge to others. Of both genders.

We may have made moves to create a greater level of financial equality over the last 50 years, but we still have a long way to go, and I don't want my daughter and her children to still be on the financial back foot as they progress through their lifetimes. I don't want them to feel that they should give something up, just as it starts to get successful, or that they have to give up on their dreams, of trailblazing, and loving life.

We all have positive influences in our lives. I didn't really appreciate how "different" both my Grandmothers were, because they had just always been that way to me.

Likewise, we all have negative money stories – my own mum wasn't able to be financially independent when she found herself pregnant at 19, because society, and the financial system, still didn't allow it.

Again, I didn't appreciate this, or the challenges she faced. But now I know, it does explain some of the financial attitudes that I adopted and continue to carry with me.

The generations before us HAVE made a difference. They have all been role models in their way and, likewise, we are role models to those who come along after us.

In my "third age" I'm finally making that difference – the one I had hoped would come during my "official" financial career. Come join me! I am passionate about creating a movement that gets women confident around their finances. No guilt. No expectation, and certainly no such thing as "being no good with money".

We all have that responsibility to pave the way for our daughters, grand-daughters, nieces and God-daughters. And if you're personally in any doubt as to what you can provide of use, I'd invite you just to look back at your own lineage…you might just be inspired!

CHAPTER 5

Leverage Your Wealth Through an Online Business

KYLIE ANDERSON

Online Business Strategist & Founder Iconic Wealth for Women

"The reason I've been able to be so financially successful is my focus has never, ever for one minute been money."

Oprah Winfrey

Iconic Wealth for Women is finally unleashed into the world. It has been a desire of mine to create this book and build the community for the last 8 years, because I've met so many incredibly talented women during the course of my career and business who struggle with their finances and connect it a lot of the time to their self-worth (grrrrr!) – whether that's been around creating more income, charging what they are truly worth or building long term wealth. One thing I immediately noticed when building this community is the word "wealth" itself triggers so many women in different ways. Some positive and some negative. What does "wealth" mean to you?

For me it's all about empowering women to take control of their own finances, to have independence and to have freedom of choice.

Who am I to talk to you about this?

Well let me take you back a bit to when I was just 27 years old. I stood in my bathroom, staring at a negative pregnancy test for the second time and I knew things had to change. Life just wasn't going in the direction I wanted it to and somehow the universe was pulling me to do something different.

So I went online and booked my first holiday overseas. The first time I stepped on a plane I felt like I was doing something just for me. I couldn't ever remember that feeling before..

After losing my brother at the young age of 21, then getting married at 23 and divorced by 24 (after 6 years together he cheated on me with a girl from his work!) then falling into another relationship. I felt like I had been out of control for so long.

Just going through the motions day in and day out. Not really being a part of events, just doing what everyone else wanted!

Of course I know now, that when we are living our lives to someone else's expectations then we are in complete misalignment with our soul's purpose and things feel "off" but we may not know or understand why.

When I stepped on to that plane, I knew that what I wanted was some independence, some space after all the tragedy and heartache I had suffered. I wanted some time out, time to find me, to understand who I really was and what I really wanted in life.

Travel was exciting for me. I had the Bug! I loved the different cultures and stepping out of my comfort zone. It fuelled my passion for independence and building the life I truly desired. I then stepped into my first ever sales role (I had to pay for all the holidays somehow!) It was time to get paid well for all my hard work and I smashed it. Moving up to Sales Manager in under 2 years. Leading a West London estate agency. I never looked back!

Now I really knew how to build income AND grow my wealth.

I was consistently hitting sales targets (doing millions of dollars in sales), getting paid exceptionally well and enjoying the daily challenges. But after nearly 13 years in both real estate and recruitment the hours were taking their toll on me. I never stopped!

The constant pressure to hit targets, the crazy early train commutes and long hours every day, left me with little to no personal life. And what life I did lead generally revolved around work and drinking! Ever heard the saying "work hard – play hard"? Well, that was me! I was always the life and soul of the party. But it was starting to take its toll on me.

I was feeling the burn!

I was also getting restless. I was beginning to resent building someone else's business and having to beg to take holidays, or to book a day off for something I needed. I had no life anymore. It all revolved around work and I wasn't getting any younger!

One morning my boss came into work bragging about getting his travel card – yep, that means he was at retirement age, working long hours and still coming into the office every day.

This was my wake up call. I realised I could end up like him if I kept going on the current route I was on.

I wanted something different!

So I started to look around at other options. This took me to the National Achievers Congress, a huge multi-speaker event in London where I was sitting in the crowd with hundreds of other people who wanted more! (Maybe you've experienced this yourself?)

I soon realised there was this whole world out there I hadn't even considered – like property investment, online businesses, trading, and so on. I looked at the variety of opportunities and:

- I didn't think I had the time for property at this stage and
- I learnt to forex trade – loved it, but didn't really like being stuck behind a screen without "people interaction". (And actually my broker went into receivership overnight and I nearly lost everything…but that's a story for another time.)
- I decided to embrace the online business world as I loved the leverage it had!

I started learning all about internet marketing with some of the best names in the industry like Frank Kern, Neil Patel and so on. But the field I had gotten into was a bit too "get rich quick" for me.

I started to wonder how I could use this knowledge to impact and help service-based businesses to grow online so they could have more time and create additional income streams.

I was great at spotting opportunities in businesses to create more cash flow (at one stage I even got known as the Cashflow Queen), creating online businesses and helping them to implement fast! I had the knack for taking all the knowledge and skills out of someone's heads, putting it down on paper in a structured and simplified way (creating what I call a signature program/methodology) and helping them to launch with systems that they can use over and over again to then scale!

Now why am I telling you all this…?

As an Online Strategist and Award Winning Business Coach my zone of genius is helping you build a 6/7 Figure Online Business to increase your cash flow and add recurring revenue so you have EXTRA money to build your long term wealth.

Think about it – how do you make £100,000? Sell a product/service at:

2,000 x £50

200 x £500

100 x £1,000

10 x £10,000

Whichever way you want to do it, whether you want to be more "Netflix style" or more "boutique" – you can build online income.

Have you ever realised how much knowledge and skills you have accumulated over your lifetime?

This could be through the work you've done, the experiences you've been through or even a side passion that has captured your interest.

Whatever it may be, **there is an opportunity for you to sell it online.**

I've seen examples and also had clients from so many different backgrounds take their existing skills and knowledge and create additional revenue online.

Here are just a few of my favourites:

- An awesome property client who helps you start in property with a small amount of money and secure your first rent2rent deal to create more cash flow – called "Rent2Rent Success" (created over £500k in just 3 years)

- A Financial Planner who created "the Wealth Canvas" to help her clients bring their retirement into today.

- A real estate professional in Dubai who helps people grow through social media – created "The Social Millionaire" to help others stand out from the crowd and secure more clients.

- A lady in London who created a membership around her passion for theatre. More Famous ones like Marie Kondo who helps you get organised!

You name it, someone has sold it online!

You see other people need your skills. What you do naturally others often struggle to do... and they are willing to pay for you to help them!

Why is there such a big opportunity right now?

Well the e-Learning and online education market is opening up even more opportunities as it's set to grow to $1 Trillion by 2028! (that's a pretty big pie to take a slice from!)

Plus...

According to iPEC, 1.5 million searches are made every month by people and companies looking for life coaches, business coaches, and executive coaches.

In 2019, the estimated global revenue from coaching was 2.849 billion USD. (2020 ICF Global Coaching Study) and growing! So more and more people are looking for support to achieve their goals.

There are growing opportunities every day to build your business online and I'd love to share with you how you can do it in 4 simple steps.

But first, why do I LOVE online businesses? Because...
- Everyone has valuable knowledge and skills that are saleable
- Low Start Up Costs & High Margins
- Create Assets & Get Paid Over & Over Again
- Offers Incredible Scalability
- One of fastest path to cash flow
- Location Independent
- You get paid to be YOU!

If you want to grow your long-term wealth, creating an online business is one of the fastest ways to create additional cash flow and build recurring revenue.

It has allowed me to travel the world, work with amazing clients and create an incredible life for myself and my family.

Since starting I've now gone on to build a multi six figure online business (without millions of clients), and I've helped various clients create and launch their own programs as well. Without all the tech hassle, fear of sales and overwhelm!

You might be asking – how do you get started?

After working with clients over and over again, helping them to launch and grow their online businesses, I slowly started to create my own system for success.

This consists of Four Core Pillars to building a successful online business:

PLAN

It all starts with having the right foundations in place AND creating your PLAN.. Firstly, you have to understand your PROBLEM SOLVING IDEA (how you help them). Then having complete clarity on your IDEAL TARGET MARKET (who you'll sell to) and how you can help them. Before starting to create your brand and content strategy to become the EXPERT AUTHORITY in your industry with your own unique selling points (USP) so they only want to work with you.

PACKAGE

Now that you have the foundations in place it's time to PACKAGE YOU UP.... and define a business model to suit your LIFESTYLE and to generate the desired INCOME you want. (One Size Doesn't Fit all!) I'll show you how to extract your knowledge (out of your head) and create a CORE SIGNATURE program (your own methodology). Then we want to define your BUSINESS MODEL that gives you the freedom and ability to scale. Then design your SALES process to attract clients on a consistent basis who are not only willing to pay you, but do the work as well.

PROMOTE

With your knowledge unpacked, it's time to CREATE AN IRRESISTIBLE OFFER, understanding the PRICING & BONUS structure you will use to get paid what you are worth, whilst still having clients begging you to join. Before it's time to start that LAUNCH process so you can not only test your content, but get your FIRST CLIENTS too.

I love the feeling of getting your first online client – when you do it once, you can repeat it over and over again!

PROFIT

Now that your first launch has been created and you are selling your program. it's time to start to think about how you can really profit from your signature program (methodology).

The first step is to make sure you DELIVER an awesome program. Your first program is the most important part of your 6-figure income growth (as you want those glowing testimonials)

From there it's time to SYSTEMISE the process around "selling" your program so you can handle taking on more clients with ease.

Once these are in place, it's time to really grow and that means increased VISIBILITY – gaining things like publicity and getting in front of other people's audiences to expand your reach fast!

And remember the most important part to all of this is to really understand the Problem You Solve and the Result it brings to your ideal audience.

One of my favourite sayings is always, "Sell the holiday, don't sell the plane."

People buy the outcome and the results you can get them (and how you make them feel), especially when buying higher ticket courses and programs.

The goal is to save your clients' time, money and emotional stress which they would incur if they went on their own journey without your help.

The three most profitable areas for building online businesses are where you solve problems associated with: Health, Wealth & Relationships

If you can connect your expertise to helping solve one of these core problems, you are more likely to succeed.

Going online to create a course or program doesn't just give you additional revenue or recurring cash flow, it can also help you:

- Bring in High Quality Clients.

- Grow your list for future revenue growth and adaptability.
- Position you as the expert in your industry!
- Reach a wider audience base!
- And open up more opportunities like speaking, podcasting and so on!

Stuck for an idea to get started with?

You might even be sitting there thinking – **what could I possibly do or help people with?** – I'm not a guru/expert! (One of the most common things I hear from highly experienced people....)

So I want you to have a little brainstorming session to get your creative juices flowing – and remember we all have knowledge and skills that someone else would pay for – and most of the time it's the "most obvious" to others but not to us!.

On a blank piece of paper (I love coloured pens and mind maps....) make a cross down the middle of the page and across the page to create 4 Segments.

In each area start to jot down ideas that relate to the following core themes:

WHAT YOU DO! – this is teaching or helping them with what you do now –

eg. if you are a web designer – this is actually how to build a website for themselves.

Or an interior designer – how to design a room to attract awesome tenants. You get the drift I'm sure.

WHAT YOU KNOW! – this is more around how you got to where you are today.

eg. How did you build a successful design business? How did you get started, attracting clients and so on?

WHAT YOU'VE EXPERIENCED – have you overcome something or experienced something you can now help someone else with?

eg. Have you lost loads of weight? Have you travelled cheaply? Maybe you've eliminated debt and have a way to help others do the same.

WHAT YOU ARE PASSIONATE ABOUT – maybe you have a side passion, that you just love, you could build a community around.

eg. A lady in London built a community around theatre – swapping tickets, sharing events, interviewing people in the industry and so on. It was her passion.

I know people that have built sites around nail painting, cleaning, knitting, gardening and so on. What are you passionate about that you could talk about every day?

I hope that has got the cogs turning and your creative juices flowing. There are so many opportunities to grow additional income online. BUT it still takes work and commitment, so be prepared to put some time and effort in (and ignore the overnight success stories!!!) to enjoy the leverage and growth opportunities which are endless.

And remember you are probably reading this book to grow your long term wealth and one thing I do know is that building any type of assets will help you create recurring revenue and increased cash flow so you can invest more! We all need more money right?

So whatever wealth vehicle you choose, make sure you **BUILD or ACQUIRE ASSETS** – Courses, Books, Programs, Lists, Podcasts and so many more!

And remember my saying – **"If good women earn good money, they do good things."** It's your time to create more income, impact and influence.

Want to find out more about building a 6 Figure (Plus) Online Business feel free to connect with me. You'll find me as the Founder and host of the Iconic Wealth for Women Community, on the Iconic Wealth for Women podcast and if you are ready to get started building an online business my free guide – **4 Steps to Launching Your Online Program can help you get started – https://bit.ly/guide-htsp**

CHAPTER 6

Lessons I've Learned – Building Wealth Through Business to Create Abundance, Fulfilment and Legacy!

LAURA PARR

Conscious Business Strategist

Wealth is a fascinating topic. Most people immediately jump to assuming wealth means money. When we refer to wealthy people, we're talking about the ones with the big houses and always on vacation to extravagant and exotic climes.

But this isn't actually the case. Wealth is so much more than that. Wealth incorporates money, yes, but it also refers to your level of fulfilment, happiness and purpose.

And this is starting to become more apparent to people. Whether it's down to Covid for showing us that there really were alternative ways to live that didn't involve slogging it out in an office doing a job we didn't like, or the change in how we outwardly value mental health as a nation, the scripts are being re-written and people are waking up to the fact that money isn't everything if we aren't living a life that's true to what we want and who we are.

This has led to millions leaving the world of employment – in the last few years it's been in droves! Heading out into the entrepreneurial landscape seeking that illustrious promise of autonomy, freedom and financial abundance.

So why is it then that 20% of all companies started, fail in their first year? By 3 years, that's up to 60% according to a Fundsquire survey. That's a huge percentage!

Well, for most people, the focus is still on an almost desperation to create money! For money is the provider of all those things that we think we want and need in order to make us happy.

And herein lies the issue. Businesses are NOT just a vehicle to make us rich. Sure, they can do. But if the motivation and purpose of starting a business is just on how much it will make, it will never be sustained long term. Being an entrepreneur can be hard at times, and if you don't love what you do, and if it doesn't align with what you want out of life, then money is not a strong enough motivator to keep you going. It never is. You may think it is, but when it actually comes down to it, it's the value you've attached to what the money will provide you that is more motivating to you.

There's no point in starting a business to allow you to be at home with your kids, or travel the world, if it then scales to something that you have to manage 100 hours a week and haven't built to leverage out easily.

Knowing the foundations of your wealth model – your values, your purpose, what you want from life – is crucial to beating that statistic and building a business that brings you long-term fulfilment and success for decades to come, should you want it to.

And the irony is that the more you enjoy and find fulfilment in your business, the more money you're actually likely to make anyway!

But it's these foundations that most entrepreneurs skip. They're chasing the short-term cash, and in a society of instant gratification, we just want to get going and make those millions we see so many others making.

For most women I work with, giving back and knowing that they are building and leaving a legacy for their kids, family, or the world at large, is something very key to activating the fulfilment aspect of true wealth in their lives.

As a business coach and mentor, I specialise in helping women to create businesses that combine their desire for financial wealth, autonomy, fulfilment and giving back, by incorporating elements of social, environmental or economic return in their business structures. Social impact used to be a luxury or simply a marketing ploy for companies, and the concept of philanthropy was something only done by the rich. But now, it's becoming a business necessity.

People's buying decisions have increasingly, and quite rapidly moved towards being based more on a business' social footprint and impact. Setting up something that allows your business to be a vehicle for social or environmental change whilst also providing you all your personal needs and wants as well, is categorically the future of commerce.

For me, I've learnt this through personal experience. I started out my working life in the corporate world – I got a job at one of the world's largest consulting firms straight out of studying business and economics at university. I'll be honest, I didn't really know what I wanted to do, but the university were pushing these high end jobs as being the most prestigious result of getting good grades from your degree and the salary was one of the best graduate ones around. So why not.

It didn't take long for me to realise that this was not my scene. I thoroughly enjoyed the people I worked with, but found the working world restrictive and not as exciting as I'd hoped having a job would be. Both my parents, for as long as I can remember, have always been self- employed as well, so I think it was innate within me that I wanted to do my own thing.

My mum also loves to recall that as a child I loved to try and sell her my drawings. Once she'd accepted once, my brain spun with ideas of how much I could make if I just sped up my working processes. This led to scribbled skies done in haste, and rejected pictures. I learnt quite quickly that quality control and high value were integral to customer retention.

So a few years later I turned to the world of property. I'd always loved property. I was that geeky kid who watched Homes Under the Hammer and revelled in the transformations that were made. I'd always loved seeing the old and outdated being made to look fresh, modern and inviting. I still do. I can spend many an hour on Pinterest looking at all the amazing kitchen & bathroom extensions people have done, despite having done ours only 2 years ago. So it seemed like a great move towards doing something I loved.

But I didn't really dig any deeper than that into the decision. Before I knew it, I'd done a couple of developments – which were fun, but so much more than just the interior design elements near the end – and had started a property management company that specialised in guaranteed rents. This was a sound business decision in my industry at the time, and the model for expansion and growth was clear and easy to follow. But 10 years down the line, I hated it. With fiery passion.

I was exhausted by the work and everything I had gone through to get the company to where it was. It felt like so much had been against me – with regulation changes that meant I had to make huge changes, costing thousands of pounds and losing me some of my business, to immensely challenging tenants and unscrupulous partners along the way. I watched so many people with far less experience & expertise build the same business, faster and seemingly easier. And yet the thought of picking myself out of this rut and doing the work to do the same was unthinkable. I had done well and built a big business, but I'd lost all love for it and was left entirely uninspired and fed up.

Unintentionally, I'd followed the money. The business model made clear sense – it still does. But in hating it, I was never going to be a big player in this game and frankly, by that point, I didn't want to be.

So this started me on my journey of self-discovery. I'd always been fascinated in personal development and psychology, and I started to really analyse for myself what I found important. What I wanted out of life. What life actually *meant* for me. And why it was that I had made the decisions I had. I didn't know it, but I was essentially defining what wealth meant to me and where I wanted to take it from there.

And that's what led me to business coaching and specialising in helping women create socially and environmentally conscious businesses. I love to teach. I love to help. I'm also one of those weird people who love public speaking. And I realised how important it was for me to feel like I was leaving the world somewhat better for me being here.

It's true that one person can't, on their own, solve all the world's problems, but by coaching, training and spreading the concept of what I call conscious business models, I hope to inspire so many others to each do their own bit. And so, I am building myself a network of amazing women doing amazing things, all of which help so many incredible causes, from supporting and advocating for equal rights, to providing opportunity to those without, to reforesting the planet and clearing the oceans. All while allowing them to spend more time with family and doing what they love. In business terms, it's my ultimate leverage to solving the world's problems. In human terms, it fills my soul with so much joy, inspires me every day and provides the lifestyle that I'd always wanted for myself and my family at the same time.

So how can you do the same?

Maybe you've been thinking about starting your own business as part of your journey to personal wealth. Fantastic! Especially if you also want to use it to create your legacy and as a tool for fulfilment as well as financial wealth. But perhaps here is where you get paralysed by questions and fears such as how do I even start? How is it that you combine the two? Is it really possible for me to do this? I don't have a business background/not sure what my true purpose is.

Well firstly, yes. You absolutely can do this! My first piece of advice is to make sure you don't do any of this on your own. Entrepreneurship can be notoriously lonely, but support and guidance doesn't just satisfy your need for social interaction – it's incredibly important to achieving solid success, and faster too. Don't reinvent the wheel. Learn from those who have done what you want to do. I wish I had done this sooner.

And secondly, I'm going to let you in on my 4 Pillars of Success! I use this model with all my clients in order to help them work towards a solid and sustainable business plan, built on foundations stronger than steel.

PILLAR 1 – CLARITY

Firstly, get clear on your vision and purpose. Start out by doing some personal exploration into your highest values and what you truly want out of life. This will give you the basis for knowing where you want your business to take you and equally importantly – why. Why are you here on this earth? What is your gift? What is the legacy that you want to leave?

PILLAR 2 – CONNECTION

Then connect with your marketplace and ideal audience. Great businesses solve a problem – make sure you know what your market wants and clarify what the problem actually is! Are you solving it, or are you solving your own problem? Who else offers what you do? Why are you better?

PILLAR 3 – CONSTRUCT

How are you going to structure the business so that it works for you and gives back socially or environmentally? There are so many great examples of this worldwide – get inspired by looking at how so many others have done it before you.

Some of my favourites include Elvis & Kresse who manufacture luxury handbags and homeware from decommissioned fire hoses and other items destined for landfill. The great thing about them is that they defy the misconception that 2nd hand or recommissioned products have to be cheap or of average quality, relying more on the moral aspect of saving the planet to get sales rather than the quality of the actual good itself. They're beautiful.

Then there's Tentree who are an apparel company who commit to planting 10 trees for every item you purchase from them. Radiant cleaners only employ ex-offenders, ex-homeless, survivors of domestic abuse etc. Grameen bank is a Nobel prize winning microfinance bank that offers loans to the poorest people in India who don't have the credit rating or collateral to get any other form of financial help, offering them the chance to work themselves out of poverty by providing much needed funding for business start-ups. They have one of the highest payback records of any bank globally & have been rightfully recognised for their incredible work.

Don't be overwhelmed by these examples – you can start small. Mother Theresa didn't know the legacy she was destined to create. She just wanted to help a few people on the streets who needed some extra love. You have no idea what you will grow from a small action. I know of accountants and chiropractors who run a regular practice but commit to supporting a particular regeneration project locally or overseas for every client they onboard. It's simple, it's easy to implement and it still creates an impact.

PILLAR 4 – COMMITMENT

Make it happen! Work out what the barriers are to achieving your desired results, plan out your business goals for your first year at least, and then take it step by step. Rome wasn't built in a day, but by god I bet the Romans were glad they put that first brick down.

So I hope this helps to give you some inspiration as to how you can use business to build a sustainable and holistic level of wealth that goes far beyond just financial gains, but also encompasses all those life fulfilling aspects we all desire – legacy, happiness, freedom and choice.

It is your right to all the wealth you desire. Use all the chapters in this book to guide you on your way, and do whatever it takes to create exactly what you want in life! And if you need help and guidance, you know exactly where we all are. Working together to create more is smart. And I can't wait to hear of some of the stories our readers have in their journey to wealth and prosperity.

If you want to find out more about how to start and scale your own Conscious Business then I am the founder and host of the Conscious

Business Community Facebook group, the Conscious Business podcast which can also be found on YouTube and all my socials, and if you would like some more inspiration as to what a conscious business could look like then you can download my free guide – How to combine Passion with Profit to create a business of Freedom and Purpose where I detail 5 ways you can make this happen!

Guide here: Bit.ly/passion-profits

CHAPTER 7

Money, Money, Money…

LESLEY THOMAS

Founder – The Money Confidence Academy®

'Money, money, money, oh so funny in a rich man's World'.....Don't you just love a bit of Abba...but sometimes even they got it wrong...This song has so much to love about it, a catchy tune, a great chorus...but a terrible message.....if you want to be wealthy, you have to marry a rich man, or win big through gambling....umm I don't think so!

This song may have been released in the 1970s, but so much of many women's relationship with money, their money mindset, is still very much reflected in this song today. They believe that no matter how hard they work, they will never have enough money, that wealth is for someone else, because they are simply not deserving or capable enough, to build wealth for themselves.

Yes in 2023, this is still a set of limiting beliefs held by so many women and it is THIS that is holding them back, not a lack of opportunity, to prove to themselves that absolutely the opposite can be true!

We know through many years of research on the subject, that our limiting beliefs, about ourselves and our relationship with money, are formed largely between the ages of 0 and 7.

Some people might say that they can't remember what happened to them, before the ages of 3 or 4, but whilst our conscious minds may not recall the events that led to our limiting beliefs being formed, our subconscious mind absolutely will and with certain traumatic events, or events it perceives to be traumatic, our subconscious will bury those memories for us, to quite simply protect us from reliving them.

A number of those events may not be as our subconscious mind interpreted them, but that is irrelevant to an extent, because once those limiting beliefs have developed...this starts a whole chain reaction of limiting decisions...which plot out the course of our lives, the action we take and the results that follow.

It is not the limiting beliefs that hold us back. As Nike says, 'feel the fear and do it anyway'....we can choose to adopt that approach when an opportunity presents itself to us. We see the opportunity, we feel afraid, but we do it anyway. We realise we need to put ourselves forward for something, and whilst it might terrify us, we know we must do it, as the consequences of not doing so, are either bigger, or it will end up in an opportunity lost forever. That is having a limiting belief, but consciously not allowing it to hold you back.

Alternatively there is having a limiting belief and making a limiting decision, which results in you not moving forward, turning down opportunities, making excuses for all the reasons why you can't and won't do something. And simply not doing it.

Let me provide examples of both these situations, to illustrate the point. Someone may hold a limiting belief, that they are not good at public speaking and as a result, make a limiting decision to never speak publicly.

They are offered an opportunity of promotion at work, but it involves presenting to those making the decision on the promotion. So this person, tells themselves, they don't want the promotion, they don't need a pay rise, they are very happy with their current role, it would involve more time spent working, it would be stressful, they simply wouldn't be offered the promotion, so why put themselves through the discomfort etc. So they simply don't apply for the promotion....and allow regret to be the emotion they revisit on a regular basis.

Or another situation, where someone also felt they were not good at public speaking, but recognised, that if they didn't do something to improve their confidence and practise the skills needed to speak well publicly, this would hinder their opportunities to progress and ultimately prevent them from being able to learn, develop and enhance their ability to make more money and own how their career progressed.

So this person decided to take action and offered to speak in team meetings and learn the skills they felt they lacked, to help increase the level of confidence they had in their abilities. When the opportunity for promotion was presented, whilst they still felt the fear.... they went for it anyway! They won the promotion, saw a healthy increase in their salary and the upscaling in their lifestyle that accompanied it.

Same situation. Same limiting belief. One example of a limiting decision being taken, as a result of that limiting belief. One example of not allowing opportunity to be limited, by that particular belief.

By the way, both those examples were real...they were me and who knows how different my life might have been today, if I had made a limiting decision and not taken intentional action.

Our limiting decisions about ourselves and our capabilities, have a direct result on our relationship with money, and a direct result on our money mindset. In fact, our money mindset is a direct reflection of our relationship with ourselves – which develops as a direct result of our sense of self-worth, self-value and self-confidence. How we do money quite simply, is how we do everything.

It's only when we realise that it is us that create our reality, based on whether we consciously or unconsciously, allow our limiting beliefs to be the reason to actively not take action, to demonstrate we can create a different reality.

To support you in gaining a better understanding of yourself and your relationship with money, let me introduce you to my ADIOS 101™ framework. ADIOS, the Spanish for goodbye, to your limiting beliefs around money and hello to increased self-value, self-worth and self-confidence.

A–Awareness

D–Desire

I–Information

O–Observation

S–Systematic

Awareness

The key to an improved relationship with money, is to create the awareness of where that relationship is right now and being really honest about where you would like it to be. Asking yourself the right questions and taking time to consider the answers and the emotions that come up as a result, is a powerful way to connect with the changes and action you will commit to as a result.

Create some time for yourself, to be able to quietly work through and reflect on each of the following questions. Journaling is such a powerful tool for self-coaching, but only when you are really honest with yourself

1) What ONE thing do you currently like about your relationship with money?

2) What ONE thing do you want to change about your relationship with money?

3) What excuses are you currently making about your relationship with money?

4) What does holding onto this excuse give you permission to do or conversely not do (remember my example above)?

5) What would happen if you could no longer use this excuse ever again, what would you do instead?

6) What is stopping you from doing (the response you gave to question 5) now?

Focus on just one area of your relationship with money initially, because to do more than one at a time, can become overwhelming and this could result in your subconscious providing feedback, that this is just too hard, too much effort and what's the point. A situation we want to avoid. So, chunking down what is happening within your Money Mindset, one piece at a time, is the secret to success.

Once you have started the process of creating change, you can start again, for the next thing you want to work on.

You want to create a pattern interrupt, which opens up your subconscious to what is possible for you, to allow it to accept why doing this work will create the evidence of why change is the right approach to take for you, and what can be achieved.

Think back to a time when you have been at your very best and achieved something that you set out to do. Spend some time thinking about how you made it happen. How did you feel when you made it happen? What surprised you during the process of achieving the outcome you were seeking and what did you learn about yourself in the process?

Desire

Next is to really understand why you want to change your relationship with money? What does your life currently look like and what elements of it are being directly impacted by your thoughts, feelings and actions (limiting decisions) around money?

How much do you want to change that relationship with money and how can you create the real emotional connection to committing to the action required to make that change actually happen?

Visualisation can play a powerful role in helping you create that real, true emotional connection, to what you want and not just that, but a feeling more powerful, than the temporary drive that motivation provides.

Motivation is usually fleeting; it doesn't create permanent change. This is why New Year's Resolutions normally fail, because you are simply acting to move away from something e.g. drinking too much over Christmas, eating too much festive food, not taking enough exercise, as opposed to really creating the desire for change. A desire so strong, that you will still lean into it, long after the initial motivation has disappeared.

When you create real, real desire, which you powerfully and emotionally connect with, a feeling so strong, that you feel excited bubbles in your stomach (the stomach is often referred to as our second brain, as it is here so many of our desires begin and end, e.g. butterflies and that 'sinking feeling'), and regularly revisit this desire and amp up those feelings of connection, this is when you will continue to take action, no matter how uncomfortable, to ensure you actually achieve the desired outcome.

Try this exercise, to really connect with your desires around money and use this as the catalyst for the change in your actions.

Paint a picture of what the next level of success looks like for you. What is your REAL dream, the BIG one? (Not the downsized version you have been accepting and telling yourself is OK for you...because of those limiting beliefs).

- What would it mean to you to be able to achieve that dream?
- Picture yourself as though you have already achieved it, and imagine what you are seeing, what you are hearing, smelling and tasting, what you are wearing, who you are hanging out with, what your daily routine looks like, what you are buying, where you are living, and how you are celebrating where you are now at.
- Really lean into how you are feeling. Amplify those feelings as much as possible, create that feeling of excitement in your stomach.
- Imagine you have a TV remote control in your hand and you are using the buttons to increase the colour, turn up the

brightness, so it is bigger, brighter and more impactful than you ever thought possible.

What can you draw on right now to actively help you to be able to live the life you created in that visualisation? What are your gifts, talents, qualifications and experience, which could help you start achieving this big dream?

Because we are not always capable of seeing our own capabilities, now is also a good time to reflect on what others have told you, you are good at. The positive feedback you have been given previously, but chosen to ignore, because when we are being hard on ourselves and our capabilities, this is when we will choose to ignore the evidence from others and continue to hold onto the limiting beliefs about ourselves— even when there is evidence to the contrary.

Remember, fight for your limitations and you get to keep them!

Information

The next step in the ADIOS 101™ framework is Information. Understanding the information that you are providing yourself that is hindering you from developing the right relationship with yourself and with money.

So much of our thoughts and feelings about ourselves are developed and reinforced through the internal conversations that we have with ourselves. It is when this conversation is not a positive one, or even destructive. This is when a sense of lack develops in how we feel about ourselves and what we are capable and worthy of achieving.

A simple but effective tool for better understanding the quality of the internal conversation we are having with ourselves, I call the 24-hour Notebook Exercise. Carry a notebook and pen around with you for 24 hours and every time a negative thought pops into your head about yourself, take your pen and notebook, and write it down. HOWEVER, don't write the thought down in the negative, write it down in the positive!

An example, 'I can't go live on Instagram, I sound rubbish'…. write down, 'I am confident, capable and will help people by going live with my story on Instagram'.

Do this every time a negative thought pops into your head that day. Firstly it will make you fully conscious of just how often you speak negatively to yourself (and awareness, remember, is the first step in creating change) and secondly, you will be creating a set of affirmations that specifically work for you, as opposed to generic ones, that may not.

Then make a daily commitment going forward, to reverse the negative internal conversation, by recognising it, mentally affirming the opposite and by consistently committing to this. Quickly you will find yourself stopping those thoughts from happening in the first place.

Observation

Next in the process is observation. Recognise how your internal thoughts and feelings about what you think and believe is possible for you is starting to shift (as a result of the first 2 steps). Make mental notes and also take physical notes, when these shifts occur, and how these turn into positive thoughts on what you feel about yourself. But even more importantly, the action that you are now taking and the results that are now showing up in your life.

Creating evidence for your subconscious that changing your thoughts, feelings and actions is safe to do, will allow your subconscious to accept that doing things differently is safe for you. Not only is it safe, but it actually produces the right results for you, will ensure your subconscious actually shows up and suggests other things for you to try.... This might be when you least expect it and were not even actually looking for a solution at that point in time...I call these my 'shower moments', due to that often happening when I have a shower.

Systematic

The final part of the process, which actually is not final at all...is systematic. This is because our relationship with ourselves, which defines our relationship with money and how that is tied to our sense of self value and self-worth, is never ever one and done. It is always a work in progress. New levels, new devils. However, once you make the commitment to the rest of the ADIOS 101™ process, I have outlined.

Awareness

Desire

Information

Observation

Then automatically, you will be able to utilise this process, to overcome any set back that up-levelling presents to you, because you now have the tools and insights to make it happen. Going forward you will be able to quickly get into action to prevent new obstacles from stopping you achieving the success you want to see. You will be able to anticipate and plan for limiting beliefs not becoming limiting decisions and be able to navigate yourself successfully through them, faster than you thought was possible.

Always remembering

Where Mindset goes, Money Flows®

Lesley is the founder of The Money Confidence Academy and host of the Let's Talk Money and more podcast – a weekly show that discusses all things money, mindset and how to turn around limiting beliefs, so that you can develop a healthy wealthy relationship with money. Lesley is here to help you to re-educate, reconnect and redefine your relationship with money to unlock your ultimate success.

CHAPTER 8

Money Makes the Love Go Round

LOUISA TRUNKS

Philanthropy Advisor and Fundraising Consultant

I love money. I talk and think about it all the time, it feels to me like Love's life-partner, pumping through the world and lighting things up. But, for me this isn't because of the material things it can deliver to my doorstep, it's because of the power it has to bring me wealth. Real wealth: the kind that fills you with a sense of contentment. Money gives me more space and time to be with my family and to have adventures, it allows me to make more healthy choices, it means I can afford things that reduce my stress and give me pleasure, that I can explore and experience more of our magnificent planet, and that I can achieve my dreams. There is one more thing too… it enables my philanthropy. I am a philanthropist and my ambitions for changing the world are intrinsic to my sense of achievement. I do not consider myself a success unless my exploits have made the world a better place for someone along the way.

A philanthropist is often thought of today as someone who donates large sums of money to good causes, but for me this definition is restrictive and exclusive. Having graduated as a classicist far too many years ago, I prefer the original, more expansive definition. In ancient Greek Philanthropy means 'Man-lover'. If we give our chauvinist ancestors a hand, and lend them a 'Hu', we come to a lovely definition of this hard to pronounce word:

A philanthropist is a lover of Humans.

Philanthropy is a commitment to loving your fellow humans (and animals and our planet) every day and doing what you can to make this world a better place. Sure, making large donations is an important part of that, money is, after all, power, but more often it's not. Sometimes my philanthropy is gifting thousands of pounds, other times it's giving 5 minutes to a man living on the street who needs to be seen and heard, or adapting my employment practices to make my neuro-diverse staff feel safe and valued. I believe Philanthropy is a way of life, it's a life of a thousand loves.

Most often, perhaps because of what I do, the women I talk to move quickly on from their money-making tales to tell me about how they want to give back, how their wealth will allow them to do what they really want to do, which is inevitably a version of 'change the world'. This is when they really light up; the talk of setting up foundations, helping people to overcome the challenges they faced in their youth, giving hope, support, opportunity and care to other humans, making our planet a better place. This human and planet loving passion seems to make us alive, it is our essence and to feed it we must – not through any sense of duty or shame, but because it seems to be at the very heart of what it is to be a woman. We create, and we love. We are all Human-lovers. We are all philanthropists.

Part of my own dream is to use my skills and experience to amplify and expedite other people's philanthropy.

I help individuals and organisations to achieve a bigger, brighter impact for people or planet via a 4 step plan:

Step 1 – Where do you want to go?

There are 3 main ways to change the world:

1. As an individual

2. Through your company

3. Via your own Not-For-Profit organisation

But these are the busy Whats, and the noisy Hows. First, must come the Why. Like with all endeavours, it's easy to get caught up in a quagmire of detail, but taking time to seek out your Why expedites your journey and amplifies your impact. Often I hear things such as 'I will set up a centre for women escaping domestic violence' or 'I want to stop our Oceans dying'. These are all worthy and valid Whats, and if you spent your life working out how to do this then some good would come, some philanthropy would be dispensed, and the world would be a little better for sure. But, I spend a good deal of my life helping people to determine their philanthropic Whys, because it's simply like adding petrol to the fire.

A workshop I ran at a Housing Association springs to mind; the room was full of experienced, intelligent, motivated support staff. We were gathered to devise their case for funding and I asked them why people should support them. A question so simple it almost annoyed the room, and tired explanations of what they did and how they did it were delivered on a wave of sighs. I gently batted each back, with a 'But, why?'. This rankled and landed as a jibe, which wasn't my intention and when the group exhausted the Whats and Hows there was an uncomfortable silence. I held it until the magic of realisation started to pour into the void. These wonderful and very passionate people started to shed the years of 'Do, Do, Do' and the stale, corporate mantras, and started to tap into their source of passion. Each of them really, deeply cared about the humans they were housing. They had a profound understanding of the complex humanity behind the statistics and they started to talk about Why they were involved. It was personal, and the group began to address each other rather than me. Through the nuances of their individual drivers a common Why emerged, and if we had been a painting, we'd have gone from our Victorian portrait to a masterpiece in Pop Art. The light was on and my work was done; the Why not only gives you direction, but it also acts as the connector. All philanthropic endeavours need to garner support; be it funders, delivery partners, advisers, or even the beneficiaries themselves. Your Why is the most powerful connector. It cuts you through the crowd to reach your people.

Your Why also feeds your vision, and determines where you want to go. I met the individual above who wanted to 'stop our Oceans dying' whilst I was setting up a Major Gift programme for a national charity. His Why was children – he believed passionately in their innate equality and wanted to create the brightest future possible for every child. He had been directing his efforts at UK Children's charities and then one of his light bulbs pinged on: What was the point if there were no habitats left on earth for these children to build their futures in? This very inspirational and generous gentleman pivoted with speed and fury, outraged at what he felt to be the ultimate injustice, the pinnacle of inequality. The Ocean's survival was critical to his vision. His Why remained the same, his What and his How changed in response to his environment and circumstance.

Another benefit to taking time to identify your Why, is that it's like a great big nose blow of philosophy, theory and beliefs. A clear out and capture of all the postulating, the hypothesising and the glorious, down the pub style rantings of 'but, it has to change, this is just so unfair'. These drivers are not to be dismissed, but having given them their God-like dues, it's time to park them, leaving them to shine as our beacon, whilst we get down to the meat of the thing: Where are you now? And how are you going to get where you want to go?

Step 2 – Where are you now?

This step is serious, it's time to put your specs on: an audit is required so that subsequent plans are built with a clear view of the foundations. It should be simple, but in my experience it rarely is: My clients are often entrepreneurial, inspirational folks who can sometimes be drowning in ideas and good intentions. Driven by passion, fired up by our work on the Why behind their philanthropic vision, there is rarely much enthusiasm for pausing to take stock. But, in my experience and opinion, those that succeed understand the need to **Go Slow to Go Fast**. An audit does not need to be onerous, but it does require the full shine of your focus, and a commitment to honest appraisal.

An audit starts to pad out the answers to the many questions you may have about your philanthropy, such as:

- How can I be philanthropic whilst I am building my wealth and have little cash to redistribute?
- Should I donate through my company? Or set up a Donor Advised Fund? Or establish a foundation?
- What is the right structure for my philanthropy to minimise admin costs?
- Is my organisation ready to fundraise? How long will it take me to raise my target?
- How can I increase the impact of my endeavours?
- Should I support a charity? Or set something up myself?
- What do I need to know to achieve my dreams? Who will I need in my Power Team?
- What are my blind spots?
- Can I do this? (Yes, always yes, but you will need some knowledge, skills and a plan – and most often a budget).
- Are the Whats and Hows in my head the best way to achieve my Why?

It's impossible to quantify the contents here, as each audit depends on you and your situation/aspiration, but these are some things to consider.

For individuals:

- Gift history
- Current wealth and resources
- Geographics – vision and wealth
- Motivations – the agency/altruism continuum
- Experience/ understanding of Not-For-Profits, impact assessment, due diligence, project management/ delivery, funding landscape, finance/budgeting, law, policies and procedures.
- Tax position
- Your network
- Your family situation and intended legacy

For organisations:

- Organisational structure and management
- Organisational Strategy and theory of change
- Budget (expenditure and income)
- Data management
- Donations history and expectations
- Fundraising admin and infrastructure
- Financial management
- Policies and procedures
- HR
- Story resources
- Impact Management
- Strengths, Weaknesses, Opportunities and Threats.

Step 3 – How will you get there?

I am one of those that loves a good plan. Not just because I get time with Excel and her lovely boxes of joy, but because it gets me where I want to go. And if it doesn't I can see why, tinker, fix, and crack back on towards my goal. Not having a plan is like setting off in the car without knowing where you are going, so that all kinds of terrible things happen, even though there is a good chance you will get there anyway:

- Because you don't know the route, you are at the mercy of Google Maps. You end up in a cul-de-sac, wasting time and energy, swearing at everyone, and generally ruining the mood. Of course, you knew not to go this way, but when you don't plan, someone else can easily take over the driving, and you are up the alley before you realise that you know the answer.

- You realise you are particularly shouty about the route error because you haven't eaten, so you stop in a service station. You've missed Gloucester services (if you take one thing from this book, it's to always plan a stop at Gloucester Services!), so it's a manky, overpriced, sugary sub that hurts more than it heals. You've spent more money, taken longer, and your destination is no closer.

- You're late, which annoys everyone, especially Grandma who paid for your fuel because your arrival was so important to her.

Grandma never funds your trip again, two of your car team decide to get the train next time, and you have a heart-attack because of the stress and poor diet. Ok, ok, that's a little dramatic. But, you get my drift: have a plan. A plan is always a basis for change. Grandma will forgive you should your lateness be because an opportunity to get something really cool for her party came up, and your car buddies will be onboard should a well communicated change of route get them to their desired destination without your hangry, 'born of lack' rants. But devising the plan is the second part of the Go Slow, that will enable you to Go Fast later. Grandma is, after all, counting on you!

There are many ways to make a plan, but mine use the following format:

WHAT: Clear objectives that are **specific** and **relevant** to your Why/ Vision, which can be **measured** and **achieved** within a certain and specified **time**-frame.

Specific **M**easurable **A**chievable **R**elevant **T**imed

HOW: Actions required to meet objectives.

WHEN: Deadlines and dependencies. Gantt charts are useful for more complex ambitions.

WHO: Who leads and who delivers; internally and externally.

BUDGET: Income and expenditure.

MONITORING: Establish metrics to monitor more complex objectives, define your review points, stick to them, and amend your plan as a result to stay on track. Consider external monitoring requirements where appropriate, and above all be honest with yourself and review progress accurately. The power of compounding can work against you too, if something isn't right, fix it quickly.

Step 4 – Let's make it happen

It's time to Go Fast. With a clear idea of where you are heading, an honest appraisal of your starting point, and a SMART plan, you are ready to go. I love this bit – it feels like being in a nuclear reactor with explosions of potential happening all around, and the energy of that combined with your passion can make you feel giddy with excitement as you realise your philanthropic dreams are truly within your means to achieve.

I would always recommend having someone to be accountable to, and depending on how you are achieving this it may well be a legal requirement i.e. trustees. In amongst all the fun, excitement and hard work, it's easy to get side-tracked or lost, or to clunk your head against an obstacle that feels immovable. Either find a mentor, pay for coaching, or find an accountability buddy. If you have trustees or a non-executive board, use them. Welcome their different perspectives and appetites for risk, lean on them for contacts, ideas and support, and be rigorous in your collective objective/impact monitoring. Don't assume that because it feels good it's working, and equally, don't assume that because your head is sore from all the obstacle clunking that it isn't working.

If you are reading this book you are probably an entrepreneur, even if you don't call yourself one yet! Entrepreneurs make particularly good philanthropists. We dream big, think outside the box, and talk solutions not problems. We have lots of ideas. We also all have days when we know we were born to Go Big, and days when we wonder what on earth we were thinking. Sometimes you will feel like the whole world just jolted at the change your efforts made, and other times you will notice others and think your actions pale into insignificance. But, keep going. If your philanthropy leads to just one Human-Loving episode, and their world changes for the better, you're doing good. If health and energy allow, then dream big. Seize your place in this world as a Philanthropist, define your Big Fat Philanthropic Dream and then go get it. Give me a shout if I can help, you will find me on Linked In getting excited and working towards my own dreams.

Your next steps...

1. Visit Gloucester Services.

2. Call yourself a philanthropist: My name is Louisa, and I am a Philanthropist.

3. Make a commitment to do something philanthropic every single day; some days that will be a kind-eye smile to a woman who is losing her shit at the till, other days it might be a whopping donation to a charity of your choice.

4. Work on your Why. Everything starts here. Watch Simon Sinek's TED talk on the importance of Why, and then message me 'I want to play the game of 7 Whys' on Linked In. I will ask you the Question 'What change do you want to see most in the world?', then I'm going to ask you 'Why?' 7 times. It's hard, and you might even get cross, but as we peel back the layers you will start to uncover your core belief and Why you want to affect such a change. Then you can hold your Why like a cherished little baby, raise it up to the Gods of intention, thank every living thing you have what it takes to make this happen. MAKE A PLAN, and go out and make your philanthropic dream a reality.

Louisa Trunks is a Fundraising and Strategy Consultant, a Philanthropy Advisor, Co-founder of The Greenway Property Group, a Trustee of the Chapel and York UK Foundation, and a WAM Youth mentor.

Born and raised in Somerset, the land of the Summer People, Louisa now lives next door in Gloucestershire, UK, with her family. When not working or raising funds she can be found outside adventuring or enjoying a pint of real ale with family and friends. Above all Louisa values honesty, efficiency, kindness, and friendship – she will always go the extra mile to fulfil a promise. She has a blog, where she talks about her experience of cancer and survival, and she runs a lot too, slowly, just because she can.

www.linkedin.com/in/louisatrunks

www.etphilanthropy.co.uk

www.greenwayproperty.co.uk

https://newshinyoldfaithful.wordpress.com

CHAPTER 9

Levelling up Your Financial Control

LOUISA WILLCOX
Bookkeeping and Money Strategist

Money, there's something so simple about it. It's just a coin, a piece of metal or a piece of paper – let's face it. There shouldn't really be anything valuable about it. Yet it's true what they say – money makes the world go around!

Some people have lots of money, some none, and some sit in between the rich and the poor. The thing is, there's plenty to go around so why is it some of us have more than others? Why is it that as women we have such a lack of understanding around these pieces of metal and paper?

Talking about money, especially in the UK is seen as 'distasteful,' you are bragging or have far too much if you discuss your savings. Oh gosh, you want to know how much I earn a month? How dare you ask? I cannot possibly tell you something so private…but oh wait… yes we did, we had sex last night and oh let me tell you the details!

Crazy huh? Why is it we view talking about money as a sin and yet we openly talk about sex. Surely this should be the other way around.

The thing is, the way we view money is often learnt from what we see, have heard or are told, growing up. We are told not to discuss finances and to keep them private – so we do.

But, the problem with this is, we are not helping ourselves or each other in the process. We need to rid ourselves of this notion that talking about money is dirty and start speaking up and discussing our finances. Be open, honest and be willing to adapt and thrive.

It is ok to have money and it is equally ok to not have any. The place we are in today does not determine where we will be tomorrow.

I am so passionate about talking about money, I am not a millionaire – far from it. I am just an average 29-year-old woman speaking up about finances. I run two businesses, am married, and have two children and a mortgage.

My aim is to help as many fellow business women to thrive. To gain financial control and security and to fully understand how money works.

Understanding money is not hard, it's the language we use around it that complicates matters – I discuss money in simple terms and do not use jargon language.

I know you're probably wondering who I am and why on earth I think I can help you! Well, the fact is, I have been in many financial situations and everything I discuss, I have implemented within my own life. My whole career from the age of 15 has been around finances and as a qualified Bookkeeper running a thriving bookkeeping business – I have lots of knowledge to share.

Before we go into the nitty gritty details, let me just step back and fully introduce myself.

My name is Louisa. I am a 29-year-old female entrepreneur. I run two businesses – the first being my Bookkeeping business and the second my Money Strategy business. I have two wonderful children, a super supportive husband. A very energetic and cheeky German Shepherd and two lazy cats.

I'm sat here in my living room typing this chapter with my dog – Riku, on the sofa next to me. He's currently got his chew and giving me the side eye because he knows he should not be chewing it on my sofa. But whilst I'm busy I will let it slide this one time – will I regret it later? – I expect so!

The Christmas tree is lit up and my living room is decorated ready for the big day. I have clothes all over the house drying and my feet are propped up on our coffee table. I'm wearing my Minnie Mouse hoodie and my Minnie Mouse slippers (you can tell I'm a fan, right).

I own a three bed property with my husband, which I am very proud to call home. Life is busy and good. Not always stress free but close.

But, life was not always this way.

I became a single mum at the age of 20. My first son came into this world prematurely. Life was very hard, I was raising my son alone, whilst working full time. I lived in a council house and claimed benefits alongside working. But the expense of living and nursery bills made life a constant struggle.

I'd like to say I was living pay cheque to pay cheque, but the truth of the matter is – I didn't have enough money to even do that! Money was a constant worry; I counted every penny and sometimes couldn't afford to buy myself food.

I had my family around me but I felt so lonely. I worked in the bank and had done since the age of 15 but hated the job.

Whilst on maternity leave, I realised that the only qualifications I had were GCSE's as I dropped out of college. This set me on the path to attending evening college to study as a bookkeeper!

I moved from the bank to a Monday to Friday PA role within a holiday park. This is where I met my wonderful husband.

My eldest son was diagnosed with Cerebral Palsy at the age of 18 months, with a possible alternative diagnoses of Vanishing White Matter disease (the disease being a degenerative condition).

During this time my entire life altered. Stress caused me to move into a part time role making finances even harder. Very quickly I had to learn a whole new world of being a SEN mum and had to start learning all about Cerebral Palsy and the disease.

I thankfully managed to get a part time secretarial role within an Accountant's, moving to the Bookkeeping department after about 9 months.

I wanted to change my financial situation as this was causing a huge amount of worry too. This is where I started learning to properly budget. I have always been careful with my pennies and always kept tabs on direct debits.

My husband moved in, but we wanted to buy a house together, and I knew that to do this we would need to save as hard as we could. I created a new budget and we saved everything. Finally, after a year we had enough for a deposit and bought our first house before our second son was born.

I went on maternity leave and then took a year's sabbatical to care for my eldest son, after he went through a major spinal operation (after being officially diagnosed with Cerebral Palsy, ruling out the disease at the age of 5) to enable him to walk unaided. As I was due back to work, COVID-19 hit, and the world shut down. I was made redundant from the Accountant's.

This gave me the push to set up my Bookkeeping business. I did not want to have to sacrifice time with my little ones and I was sick of having to ask to take my children to appointments.

After a year of running my Bookkeeping business I set up my Money Strategy business and my Facebook group 'Managing My Money,' to help other female entrepreneurs gain financial knowledge and clarity over their business and personal finances.

If I can go from a single mum, on benefits, working full time, living in a council house to a homeowner, running two businesses, married with two children and now the breadwinner of the family – anyone can do it!

I think it's important to give you my background, so you know, no matter your situation- it is only temporary.

This is why helping others is a passion of mine. I want to show you how to gain financial control, to achieve your life dreams and goals. It is so important to know how your money works for you. I show you how to get yourself from feeling out of touch, stressed and insecure about finances, to having control, feeling financially free and open to conversations surrounding wealth.

You are probably reading this book because you want to learn how to grow your wealth. You don't want to be stuck in the same place and you want to become the woman you are meant to be. I've been there and can help you.

There is such a fear around money. This, as I said earlier, is often because of the language surrounding it when we discuss finances.

The thing is – you need to move past this fear to take control.

As an entrepreneur running a successful business, you should be looking at your finances if not weekly, but at a minimum monthly!

One of the first things I say to clients, they need to look at their own money story. Money mindset is becoming more known now and it really is a vital step in becoming financially aware. Knowing your own money story allows you to overcome any limiting beliefs you have and allows you to fully embrace your true value.

Get a journal and write down what you think about money. How do you feel when you spend it? How do you feel when you receive it? Do you have debt – how do you feel about this?

Just remember – no matter how little or how much you have. Never feel ashamed.

If you have debt, look at your statements and remind yourself what it is you purchased, why you bought it and how at the time it made you feel. Find the positive emotions around the debt and shift your mindset form a negative view to a positive one.

Looking after your personal finances is so important. You need to know exactly how your money is working for you – you do this through budgeting!

Get your bank statements and write down all your regular payments. Write down all the money coming in, then work out what you should have left at the end of the month.

Use this to see if you can change any bills – can you call companies and lower direct debits? Are there ones you've forgotten to cancel?

Once you do this, any spare money you can look at putting it towards investing – did you know you can invest from as little as £25 a month!

When creating your budget, remember, this is not a diet – it is not restrictive. Budgeting is about being financially aware and knowing how your money is working for you. Then you can make changes when you find money is being spent on things you either forgot about, or don't need anymore.

Do make sure you budget in self-care time! This is vital and I cannot stress enough the importance of self-care. Your physical and mental health are literally the most important things in the world. No amount of money can ever buy you these.

It does not have to be a huge amount. It could simply be putting £20 back a month for lunch out with a friend once a month – just ensure you have YOU time! Especially if you have children.

It is so easy to get lost in motherhood and feel guilty spending money on yourself, I've been there and done it. Oh, how I could write a whole book on mum guilt and money shaming. STOP the guilt now. Go spend some time for you – you are human, you are more than a mum and you damn well deserve it, you fabulous woman!

Another great way of saving money is to meal plan. Not only will you save tons of money, but you will also eat healthier too.

There are so many recipes online now, you really don't need to eat out or grab takeaways all the time.

Don't worry I'm not a bore and we need to enjoy life – so yes, do plan in a treat occasionally, but try not to make it weekly.

Search for 'fakeaways' online and see what comes up. Buy yourself a slow cooker, if you don't already own one and use this to cook meals and those fakeaways. It takes off so much pressure, plus, if you work full time, you come home to a hot meal – win-win all around, right.

As a business owner it is extremely important to look after your business finances too.

To be able to properly plan and scale your business you need to be running and looking at a monthly Profit and Loss – this shows you a snapshot of how well your business is doing, and quite simply, whether it is making a profit or not.

Remember, how much profit you make determines how much you can take out of your business, thus, affecting the way you live your life. I bet you have lots of plans and ideas for the year, let's make sure you achieve them.

You need to be forecasting – this gives you a rough idea of what your finances and bills will look like in the months ahead. Creating a forecast helps you to plan for possible changes throughout the year, such as a recession or if you want to close for a period to travel, or well, do what you want to do for a while. You can create different forecasts, enabling you to create strategies to ensure your business stays running.

Cashflow is the life blood of any business. A lot of owners concentrate on profit and loss, but the truth is – cashflow is more important. Without cash in the bank – you cannot re invest and if you spend too much cash without forecasting, you risk liquidation.

My biggest wealth tip for anyone wanting to grow their wealth is to really concentrate on your money story, understand it and overcome those blocks – use this to gain a positive relationship with money which will help you realise that wealth is all around us. You can then create a plan to help you reach your financial goals.

Whilst you are doing this, really start to learn and understand about your business finances. It is vital you know how to do your own forecast and how to look after your cashflow – when your business creates profit, you start to gain clarity on how to scale and this creates an impact, not only in your business but also in your personal life.

Don't leave it all to an accountant, if you don't know how to do this yourself!

How do you know if the figures they give you are correct?

What would you do if they retired?

Make sure you can always have full control, don't solely rely on someone else.

Your business finances are very interlinked with your personal finances. At the end of the day, you set this business up to help you reach your personal desires and dreams!

So, ensure you know exactly how to look at your figures. How to use them to show you the outcome of your goals and strategy. Too many focus on a business plan and the strategy for the year, but completely forget about the financial element – and yet this is the most important part.

Louisa is the creator and community leader of 'Managing My Money,' a group on Facebook she set up to support female entrepreneurs.

She shows you how you can gain financial independence and control.

Grab my 5 tips to get on top of your business finances and get in control of your money

https://subscribepage.io/business-finances

CHAPTER 10

Want to Invest in Property, but Do It Prudently and Safely?

LOUISE REYNOLDS

The Prudent Property Investor, Director Property Venture®, MCIM, Chartered Marketer

The 2022 Times Rich List includes the 250 wealthiest people in Britain.

24% of these have 'Property' listed as their key source of wealth.

If Bricks and Mortar can be harnessed to generate wealth for the richest folk, in this electronic, online day-and-age, then it can be harnessed to generate a cornerstone of your wealth-building too.

Why is property so good at helping build wealth?

Property investment is a business and, like a business, it is possible to borrow money to invest in and to run that business. This is called leverage, and it's a powerful way to make your money go further or provide greater purchasing power.

Leverage can be good as well as bad, so it needs to be used wisely, and due consideration given to what amount of leverage is right for you. Not many forms of wealth generation enable this kind of borrowing or 'gearing'.

Why is 'leverage' a good thing?

Well for the sake of simplicity let's say you buy a property for £100k, with a mortgage for 75% of that price (this is known as 75% Loan-to-value, or a 75% LTV mortgage). This will mean you put down the deposit of 25% of the £100k, so £25k.

If you invest in an area where property prices appreciate by let's say 5% per annum, that could mean 50% capital appreciation over 10 years (on a 'simple', rather than compound percentage growth calculation). That means the £100k property could be worth £150k after 10 years. You have 'made' £50k 'profit'.

For simplicity of explanation, let's exclude all costs and assuming you haven't changed the mortgage amount over that period, your gross Return on Cash Invested (ROCI) is 200% over the ten years (£150k – £75k mortgage – £25k deposit= £50k divided by your investment of £25k x 100). Or 20% p.a.

If you invested all of the £100k of your own money, without any mortgage borrowing, you would still make £50k 'profit', but the Return on Cash invested would look very different. The ROCI would be 50% in total, or 5% p.a.

This highlights the power of leverage. You benefit from the appreciation of the total asset value that has been purchased partly with borrowed money – a mortgage. Leverage, when used correctly, can act as a multiplier of wealth. You can benefit without having put down all the money needed to invest in it.

Please note there is no guarantee this will happen, but it serves to highlight the potential property can bring as an asset class to your wealth building.

Then there is Compound interest. For simplicity's sake in the previous example I have used 'simple' interest. But in reality growth is compounded because each year the property could increase based on the original value, plus the previous year's growth.

In addition rental income from the property generates a cashflow stream that is usually added onto the Return on Cash invested calculation to arrive at a Total Investment Return.

So you might now be seeing it makes sense to build wealth through property.......... but just don't know where to start?

Are you frightened of making costly mistakes?

This might be either as a result of a past bad experience or fear is blocking you from getting started.

Or you just don't have the time?

You are a busy professional, you know you want to move your property investment plans forward but never seem to get the headroom to do it because of your job or family commitments, or both. You keep getting sucked into day-to-day life and another year passes by.

It's easy to buy a property, but it is NOT easy to buy properly and safely and in the way you want.

Want to learn how to?

In this Chapter I share my **7 Steps to Investing in Property Safely.**

But first let me give you a bit of context....

Who am I to be talking about investing in property safely? Why listen to me?

I am based in Surrey, a place many people see as a rich and affluent area. So maybe this has given me an unfair advantage?

Well actually I have had to learn and work hard over the years. I graduated with a Joint Honours Degree, which qualified me to work in the Consumer Goods and Financial Services industries. I have also worked long hours as a Management Consultant, before investing in property myself and setting up my company Property Venture® to help others do so safely.

As an experienced and seasoned professional, I understand how important business skills are to property investing. Just think, working with people to get the best out of them, think negotiating skills, think organisational and project management skills. All of these are important cornerstones of building wealth through property.

I got into property as a way of looking after my family better and providing for our future financial well-being. It was a way of earning money that wasn't directly linked to every hour or day I worked. Something that became ingrained when I worked as a management consultant. Need to meet a deadline? Work harder! Work longer hours!

That is why I am passionate about 'staying safe' and 'investing prudently' wherever possible, because it's for my family.

When I started out in property, it was challenging to find others who approached things in the same way as me. Many property companies were process-led vs relationship-led, at a time when I wanted guidance and answers without all the hype and upsell.

So that's why I am fond of authenticity and delivering genuine value. And that's how I like to help other women provide for their families and secure their financial future through property. What's more I have been quoted or featured in the press for what I have to say, for my expertise in publications like: The Sunday Times, The Daily Telegraph, Sunday Express, Evening Standard-Homes & Property, Homes Magazine, A Place in the Sun.

Want to be a prudent property investor? Here's my 7-Step model

Here is my 7 Step model that I use and my clients use, which may help you to stay 'safe' when you are investing in property too. After all, it's no good spending and/or borrowing lots of money to invest, if you haven't made sure you have done all the necessary checks and balances ..... or at least the critical ones.

Do you know what they are?

My 7 Core Steps to Investing in Property Safely are:

1. People
2. Property
3. Drivers of Value
4. Effort
5. Risk
6. Fit
7. Process

1. People

This isn't the most obvious place to start when you are investing in property. Many people automatically think it's the property you need to check out first and foremost.

Well yes that is important, but the people side of the property business can mean you become successful quicker and with less mistakes, or unfortunately vice versa.

When you don't live in the area that you invest in, it becomes harder to problem-solve as or when things arise. It is therefore prudent to 'check people out', or in formal terms conduct a level of 'Due Diligence' on the people you plan to work with.

Ideally this is before you enter into arrangements and agreements. It is harder to unravel these once you've embarked on a business relationship.

This is an oft-overlooked aspect of conducting Due Diligence, and isn't something that needs to be done just on Tradespeople, it is also about vetting the professionals you will need to use.

Solicitors, for example, are not all the same in terms of their technical skill or the level of service they provide. Take the example of an online, process-oriented, conveyancing firm that many lenders offer as part of their 'free legals' package. They are not paid a significant amount by the lenders and so deliver a commensurate service. It certainly isn't personal, nor even deadline driven. This type of service is not one that works well if you are up against tight timeframes.

2. Property

How do you de-risk?

You may be seeking regular income and if so, what is your tipping point in your financial decision making?

What is the threshold level which tips you into a 'yes' or 'no' decision? Is it 6% gross yield or more on a straight rental, or could it be less if you are buying partly for lifestyle reasons, or with capital growth in mind which may give a higher total return?

Yield, a measure of annual income relative to the property value or purchase price, can vary significantly from one geography to the next. Often city-centres are desirable, but they do not always offer the best yields. Sometimes a suburb, with lower entry level prices, can deliver better returns.

Gross yields (excluding property expenses and running costs) are quite a rudimentary measure, but do enable speedy, top-level comparisons across investments.

Healthy yields are but one part of the equation. Strong rental demand has to exist to make a property work as a business investment, not only to minimise void periods, but to ensure the rental amount can be maximised. Weak demand can lead to weaker income levels, if you haven't chosen the location correctly.

If you want to add value, what Return on Investment are you seeking for a refurbishment? Or even Return on Time? Let's not forget that a predicted Return of 25% on your Cash invested within 12 months is not the same if that project ends up taking 2 years. It halves the original projection.

Mortgage availability also impacts property values. If mortgages are hard to come by, then buyers can be squeezed out of the market, which can lead to lower liquidity or reduced transaction levels. This can hamper investing in property.

3. Drivers of a Property's Value

The value of a property is correlated with and driven by a number of factors including:

Location is a huge determinant of a property's value and its worthiness as a good investment. At a micro level, the property's location within a city, its proximity to road and rail networks and the quality of schools and major employers can be critical success factors.

Country economy and micro-economy are key factors. If local incomes rise, then housing becomes more affordable, creating not only a plentiful supply of buyers for when you come to sell, but also increasing demand and ultimately property prices. It creates a positive, cyclical dynamic. If businesses are investing locally, or growing, these are good signs that the local economy is doing well.

Capital growth can mean property prices doubling over a decade, as has been experienced in places in the UK in the past. Recent times have witnessed more modest growth, with the increased level of uncertainty around the globe. There will always be locations within the UK that perform better than others and the challenge is to find those that meet your chosen strategy and approach.

Demand – demographic factors, like a growing population leads to increased demand, or the make-up of that population.

For example, if families or individuals move from the countryside to cities seeking better paid employment, this can push up demand and ultimately property prices.

Housing supply is affected by a myriad of factors ranging from: ease of planning consent, general levels of bureaucracy, existing housing stock, the cost of building, to the proportion of buyers to renters. If demand increases, but supply doesn't, then prices tend to rise.

Infrastructure improvements or regeneration act as a driver of demand. New facilities such as roads, high-speed railways, the improvement in broadband capability that attract multinational businesses, can all buoy the local property market.

4. How Much Effort to Put In?

Are you managing property investing alongside a full-time career or as a side-income, or is this your full-time business?

The answer will determine how involved and hands-on you can be.

It may be that you need to take some pragmatic decisions and get some help if you want to make your property investment a reality.

5. What About Risk?

What is your risk profile?

Do you feel more comfortable with your investments close by so that you can oversee everything easily?

Or are you at ease with investing further afield and delegating sourcing and management, so that you can spend your time on your career or profession?

Are you experienced at property investing so don't need too much hand holding and can make decisions quickly, but just need a source of regular deals?

Or are you unsure how to go about 'doing your due diligence'?

How comfortable are you with big scale projects?

Or does starting smaller feel 'safer'?

By checking out the investment and preparing yourself properly, you can make things 'safer' for you.

6. Fit: Location, Type and Portfolio?

Which type of property investment is right for you?

Are you most comfortable with adding value to the property? That may mean re-jigging the layout or refurbishing inside or building an extension.

Which location works for your investment? City-centre or suburbs?

Suburban neighbourhoods can be strong places to invest, delivering higher yields than a city centre.

Yet decent accommodation in great cities usually have persistently strong demand.

How relevant is Portfolio fit?

Are your investments too heavily weighted to one category of property, or economic cycle?

Are you wanting to re-balance what you invest in, to gain exposure to infrastructure improvements?

Or you may feel you want to re-balance your investments across the North and South of the country?

Diversification can be a good reason to invest.

7. Process – Mitigating Process Risks

Doing your homework and researching at the right point in the buying process can have a big impact.

For example, checking out the details of a potential property you are buying early on in the process, can save time and money during the process. Something as simple as checking the Title Deeds early on, before it has got to legal scrutiny, can help clarify what a vendor or agent is saying and highlight if there are any Covenants you should be aware of.

But there are limitations. Many technical legal checks are best done right at the point of purchase, so that they are fresh and current.

At the end of the process, it is important to fully check tenants' particulars and vet them, so that you continue to safeguard your property investment.

A deal can succeed or fail because of finance, so this is something to arrange early on in the process.

In Conclusion

If there's one thing to take away from this chapter, then it is, do not underestimate the power of people to either help or hinder your plans, so spend more time on this. Remember it isn't just about the property, it's the people on your 'safe' property journey too.

Louise Reynolds is a Surrey-based developer and landlord with investment property in the UK and abroad. She discusses all things 'prudent property investing'.

She has written a fuller Guide on this available here:

'7 Steps to De-Risking Property Investment'

https://property-venture.com/investment.html

She has been quoted in the press, in publications like: The Sunday Times, The Daily Telegraph, Sunday Express, Evening Standard-Homes & Property, A Place in the Sun. She has also been interviewed on a number of Podcasts and webinars.

Louise understands all aspects of property and is well-placed to help you formulate the best strategy for you or implement your plans. She offers support in the form of Mentoring or Consultancy and at the other end of the spectrum a personal investment property sourcing service.

Want to find out more about her and what she has to say?

https://www.linkedin.com/in/louisereynolds/

https://www.facebook.com/Louise.A.Reynolds/

https://www.instagram.com/louise.a.reynolds/

CHAPTER 11

Philanthropy: The Art of Good Women Doing Good Things to Create Positive Impact

NANCI HOGAN

Philanthropy Consultant and Coach

INTRO

This chapter is central to two key core claims made by Kylie Anderson at the beginning of this book. She speaks about the reasons why women should unapologetically concern themselves with creating Iconic Wealth for Women. They are 1. "If good women earn good money, they do good things"; and 2. The statement that "…. Most of us that make and talk about money don't do it for the sake of the money….WE do it to create impact. Whether that's in our own lives, our family lives or in society!"

In a nutshell these two premises, doing good and making an impact are central to becoming female entrepreneurs as well as why philanthropy should be integral to female entrepreneurship rather than just being a nice to have or a separate something we bolt-on to our business that has little or nothing to do with our entrepreneurial journey.

Philanthropy and impact are central to why we as women desire creating Iconic Wealth in the first place. It's not accumulating money for money's sake, but accumulating money as a powerful tool—one that can be used to carve out our freedom, the freedom of our loved ones and the freedom of others in the world so all may flourish.

To counteract the misconceptions women have about philanthropy and making an impact, I have developed two primary principles that I will explore throughout this article. The first one is that philanthropy is for everyone. The second one is that everyone alive is already making an impact for good or bad. To create lasting, transformative impact in the world, it is important to become aware of the impact your life is already making and think about how you can focus on activities that leverage it even more.

OBSTACLES FOR GETTING INVOLVED IN PHILANTHROPY---THE THREE NOT ENOUGHS (LACKS)

1. I DON'T HAVE ENOUGH MONEY

After conducting many polls, I have found that the biggest obstacle to people engaging in philanthropy is the misconception that they don't have enough money. They think that philanthropy is only for wealthy people once they've achieved significant financial wealth. They believe they can't do anything philanthropic until they've made their millions.

There is a widely prevalent stereotype in the media that philanthropy is only for wealthy individuals, sports celebrities or movie stars, i.e. people like Bill Gates, Oprah or Bono. The typical story goes on to recount that these wealthy individuals set up trust funds or foundations and that distribute massive amounts of money to different charitable organisations and causes. In this stereotypical story, impact is measured solely in terms of the quantity of money one can give, i.e., giving lots of money= high impact. And, finally in this story, the protagonists generally are white, western, older men. Therefore, it is even more of a challenge for people of different genders, races, socio-economic classes and ages to view themselves as potential philanthropists.

Giving money is one way to be philanthropic. But there are others.

Philanthropy, albeit difficult at times to pronounce, is actually a very simple concept. In fact, it is very much in line with two core messages in this book; good women doing good things and the importance of creating impact over making money.

The original meaning of philanthropy in ancient Greek is descriptive. It means for the love of humanity. Philos = Love and Anthropos = humanity. This is not limited to an elite but is democratic and inclusive. Philanthropy at its most basic then involves doing anything out of a love of humanity to make individuals' lives better.

Synonyms for philanthropy are helpful as well in understanding what it is and for expanding who can engage in it and how. Some common ones include altruism, generosity, charity, beneficence and humanitarianism.

Contrary to popular belief that philanthropic activities are limited to setting up foundations and trusts or other vehicles to disburse money to worthy causes, they include the following:

1. Protests and demonstrations
2. Foundations
3. Trusts
4. Social entrepreneurship

5. Advocacy at local, national and international governmental levels
6. Running for office
7. Volunteering for a charity
8. Serving as a trustee for a charity
9. Corporate Social Responsibility projects
10. Starting or working for charities, humanitarian organisations, non-profits

Finally, there are other resources besides money to consider in terms of conducting these activities. These include giving of themselves and who they are (talents, experiences and strengths), their time, and their treasure in order to make a positive difference in the world.

In fact, the biggest resources people have to bring to the table as potential philanthropists are creativity and imagination. And this is something women entrepreneurs have in spades. To be an entrepreneur, your greatest resource is also your creativity and imagination. Also entrepreneurs are mavericks and rebels. They are risk takers who refuse to accept the status quo. Otherwise, they'd gravitate to the security and financial predictability of a well-paying job and not attempt creating a business. These are also some of the personality attributes common to successful philanthropists. Philanthropists, like entrepreneurs, are not content with the world as it is. They long to make the world a better place. They, like entrepreneurs, have a vision for creating a particular kind of future- something having to do with doing good things and making an impact.

2. I DON'T HAVE ENOUGH TIME

The second, not enough, is about lacking time.

All too often people say they don't have enough time to begin making an impact through philanthropic initiatives.

The misconception that they don't have enough time stems from several things. One of the main factors is that people think that it's all or nothing---the idea that making money and doing good are mutually exclusive. People think that they only have enough time to make money, either through a 9-5 job that along with looking after their family takes up all their waking hours, or through starting a charity or non-profit.

The reality is that making money and doing good things are not mutually exclusive. It is possible to do both. First, it is possible to create a business as an entrepreneur that creates a social good that has a positive impact. One example of this is the existence of commercially viable businesses that create solutions to deal with excess plastic being discarded into our oceans.

Let me give you a personal example. I used to think this, and I spent all my time either working for a charity or working in a full-time well-paying job. I had to learn the hard way how limiting and deadly this belief can be.

It's only been in the last five years, since starting my own business as a philanthropy coach and consultant, that I have discovered how I can make money and do good things. I am now both earning money and making an impact doing what I love. I enjoy helping individuals, organisations and communities figure out how they can make money and make an impact doing what they love, and which also gives their own lives a sense of meaning, purpose and impact.

Also, doing something philanthropic does not have to be a full-time job. It can include serving as a volunteer or trustee for your favourite charity. It doesn't have to involve becoming Mother Theresa or Mahatma Gandhi. In fact, neither of them started out to create such massive projects. It was an accumulation of actions that led to their big visions and outsize impact. Mother Theresa started her work by simply giving food, water and shelter to those on the streets of Kolkata who were dying. It grew from there.

It can be as simple as seeing a need in your community and taking one small step. For example you might want to ease the loneliness and isolation of an elderly person in your community and you have a spare iPad. Maybe your action is to donate the iPad and teach them how to use it so they can stay in touch with family and friends on FaceTime and listen to podcasts.

And finally, we always seem to find the time to do the things that are most important to us. If making a difference becomes more of a priority, we can create small habits of doing generous and random acts of kindness which don't take much time. From these, bigger things can begin to develop.

3. I AM NOT ENOUGH

A lot of people think that they are too insignificant to make an impact. They believe, wrongly, that they have nothing to offer. They argue that they lack education, skills and training in setting up a charity.

The idea that one has to immediately start a full-blown charity in order to be a philanthropist that can make a significant impact is a false one.

For better or for worse, each one of us makes an impact on the world. The first question that challenges this false belief is to reflect on whether or not our lives are having a good or a bad impact on the world. Most people are not consciously aware of the kind of impact they are already making. The second question to consider is how can I better focus my life and the things I'm involved with in order to make a higher, more leveraged impact? Are there things I should quit doing?

We all are unique people with unique skills, talents, abilities, perspectives, experiences and strengths.

Every single person alive can make a positive impact in the world. Your gift is your onlyness.

"There is a vitality, a life force, an energy, a quickening that is translated through you into action, and because there is only one you in all of time, this expression is unique. And if you block it, it will never exist through any other medium and it will be lost. The world will not have it."

Martha Graham

(dancer, choreographer and pioneer of modern dance named by Time Magazine as Dancer of the Century)

The world needs your voice, your song, your gift.

FURTHER OBSTACLES: CHOOSING AN ISSUE

There are two more obstacles I have found that keep people from beginning their journey of discovery, to becoming a philanthropist. These revolve around how to choose the social impact they want to make, i.e. what issue to focus on, and once they've chosen it, where to begin. Both perceived obstacles result in paralysis. Until they are addressed people will never start their journey of discovery.

1. TOO MANY NOTES

The first problem is, "There are too many issues to choose from. How can I pick just one?" Being overwhelmed by the enormity of the problems the world faces, means many people never do anything. The misconception here is the feeling that we must address all the world's problems. But the truth is we are only responsible for our own bit of the world, and we need to trust others to address the bits of their world they are responsible for. What do you see? Mother Teresa saw crushing poverty in India. But she began by providing food, clothing and shelter only to those she encountered in her neighbourhood in Kolkata. It grew from there.

2. IT'S TOO COMPLICATED. I DON'T KNOW WHERE TO BEGIN

The second objection people raise is that, "It's all too complicated. I don't know where to start." We are blessed, or some may say cursed, by a wealth of information about resources, the issues themselves, different pathways to take, etc. But think about how you first started your business. You knew enough to begin and with each step you took, you learned more. You learned what worked, what didn't, and you learned from your mistakes and failures. You couldn't know the next step of the journey, never mind its end without taking that first step. From there it's about taking more baby steps.

However, it can be a maze and you may need to hire a guide who's gone before you.

In the final section, I will outline the discovery process that will help you address the three lacks and the two sources of paralysis around choosing and acting on the specific issue you desire to impact.

SOME PRACTICAL SOLUTIONS: MY DISCOVERY PROCESS

To address the three not enoughs and the two questions about how to choose and advance an issue, I have created a discovery process that will provide clarity. The process helps people identify what resources they have to bring to the table and how to choose an issue to focus on that is in alignment with who they uniquely are.

I find the greatest joy in my work when it is in alignment with who I am and reflects my strengths, talents, abilities, interests, passions, vision, mission, purpose and values. Making a social impact should be fun and joyful, not something that is done out of a sense of obligation.

Below are some suggestions as to how you can practically discover what resources you bring to the table by virtue of you being uniquely you.

Also, any social impact initiative will be a reflection of your mission, purpose, vision and values. When you created your business, you probably spent time doing this. It is the same process for developing a social impact initiative, whatever form it might take. The crucial thing is that both your business and your social impact project is in alignment with your mission, purpose, vision and values. Otherwise you will find it frustrating and it will drag you down.

EXPLORING WHAT YOU ALREADY BRING TO THE TABLE

First of all, you already are an entrepreneur that is creating wealth. Developing a social impact initiative as a philanthropist uses the same set of skills. You've got this.

Furthermore, you are already creative and imaginative.

Already, you are a maverick who is bucking the status quo. Women making money and creating wealth is radical. You are already engaged in a world changing project. Too few women have been at the table. Creating iconic wealth gives you influence, and power and we shouldn't shy away from that as women. Our voices, our creativity, our perspective and our insights need to be heard. It is missing. We have power, we are already powerful. Think more about how to focus and channel your voice, your power, your influence and business, even more to create a better world.

YOU CAN TEACH OTHERS WHAT YOU'RE LEARNING AS A WEALTH CREATOR

You have expertise already in creating wealth. One thing you can focus on is the lessons you are learning as you develop your wealth so you can teach others. It's not just about getting money, it's about sharing that wealth and helping others to create wealth.

YOU CAN DISCOVER OTHER RESOURCES YOU BRING TO THE TABLE: AN INVENTORY

1. Write down what you love to do and would do for free if you could.

2. List 2-5 things that you're really good at (your strengths). Hint: if you think something comes easily to you and you can't understand why others find it so difficult, then that's a strength.

3. What achievements are you most proud of, professionally and personally? What strengths and skills did you use? What do these achievements reveal to you about which values are most important to you?

4. What is the common theme that unites all these achievements, the golden thread? This will give you insight into your purpose. Anything you do to make a social impact should be in alignment with your purpose.

ACTION YOU CAN TAKE IMMEDIATELY

A good place to start is to decide on what complex social injustice issue you want to make an impact on for the better. Here are some questions to guide you.

1. **Is there a particular issue that makes you angry?**

   Anger is a good indication of your values and the areas you long to see changed. You can turn this anger into action. Recent issues involve the #MeToo movement (sexual harassment in the workplace, #BLM (Black Lives Matter which pertains to racial discrimination), or domestic abuse. Another issue is climate change.

2. **Have you or a loved one experienced an unexpected loss or change in circumstance?**

   For example, have you or a loved one recently experienced a terminal illness or lost someone due to an accident, neglect, or some preventable circumstance? I know one woman who lost one of her children. There were insufficient resources available for her family and surviving children to deal with the bereavement. She initially started a charity to locate and curate existing resources for families who were bereaved to help them cope with their loss. When my mother died of pancreatic cancer, I gave to pancreatic cancer research for a few years.

3. **Have you noticed a gap in social services in your community?**

One person I interviewed from New Delhi, India began his social impact journey when he and a fellow MBA student observed that immigrant children to New Delhi from a neighbouring rural province were unable to enrol in school in New Delhi. The problem was they had to have a certain level of education before they could enrol but they had received no formal education in their own province before immigrating. He and his friend developed a program to teach these children basic literacy and numeracy skills so they could later enrol in further education in New Delhi that would equip them to pursue a career that would take them out of poverty.

WEALTH TIP

As you build your business don't wait to give back. Explore how you can incorporate giving back in the core values of your business and practise it from the very beginning. If you wait until your business is established, you'll likely never do it. Also, this alignment between your business and your social impact initiative will create synergy which is greater than the sum of the parts. You'll end up creating greater wealth and impact by doing this.

CHAPTER 12

Anxiety, Finding Your Purpose and the Power of Your Mind!

NICKY PRICE
Transformational Therapist & Mindset Coach

The alarm went off and my favourite radio station blurted out the usual cheery messages. For a brief moment I smiled at what they were saying and then this was quickly replaced by the same sinking feeling in the pit of my stomach that had become familiar over the past few weeks.

Today it felt different. Today it felt heavier than normal. Today it felt like these awful low level anxious feelings were winning the battle that was going on inside me and I wanted to just close my eyes again, turn off the radio and hide under the duvet.

But I couldn't.

So I lay there for a few moments and wondered if THIS was the lowest point in my life.

Always an early riser and a generally positive person, the very fact that I didn't want to get out of bed made me feel scared of this all-encompassing grief and anxiety that seemed to be taking over my life. I was fearful of everything, I blamed myself, and now all I wanted to do was to shut the world out including my family and friends, in the hope that I could just deal with it and be fine again.

But my daughter needed a lift to school and the dog was waiting expectantly for his walk over the fields, so I reached out for my phone and listened to a calming meditation that a well- meaning friend had sent me. I didn't think it helped much, but with a heavy heart and a ton of effort, I managed to pull myself out of bed, drag a comb through my hair and push down the unsettling feelings to face the day.....

6 months before...

To the outside world I had a great life. A lovely home, great friends, a husband and 2 amazing teenage children and our gorgeous chocolate Labrador Archie. I had worked in a well-paid job in Corporate IT management for the past 25 years and they had even created a part time role for me after I had my children (which had enabled me to start building a digital marketing business on the side as my exit plan from Corporate life).

Life was good – and I had a lot to be grateful for, but I was starting to feel like something was missing from my life. I felt a bit disconnected and I kept having these feelings that I wasn't really "living" my life to the full or fulfilling my purpose and that time was running out for me as I had recently turned 50.

But then I felt guilty for feeling these feelings, when I already had so much in my life, but I couldn't seem to push them away.

A deciding moment arrived as the IT Company I had worked with for many years offered the opportunity of redundancy or going back full time. This felt a perfect opportunity to make the leap into full time business owner.

My digital marketing business had been doing well and I was loving the freedom of having my own business, being accountable only to ME and I was confident that with the extra focus, it would soon be a full-time income.

But right after I gave up my job (which I realised had been my '*comfort blanket*' of security), something strange happened.

My mindset seemed to shift and I realised that the digital marketing business I was building no longer excited me either and I was feeling completely misaligned to what I was doing. The feeling that I was '*here for more*' got stronger. I was *bored* with what I was doing, I was procrastinating about doing the work I needed to do and I kept **avoiding** the painful truth that the income was starting to slide away from me along with my redundancy money too.

I have this theory that when you are not in alignment with what you're doing, then the Universe starts to give you some nudges. The 'nudges' were subtle and had been showing up in my feelings, but when you don't pay attention to the nudges, then the Universe steps up and gives you a bit of a shake-up.

And that's exactly what happened.

The next 6 months I almost felt like I was on a bungee jump – bouncing perilously close to losing everything with the occasional flip and burst of energy to try and put things right in my business and build the income. But it was no use.... for the first time I slid into debt in my business and my redundancy money was all but gone.

Then came a diagnosis of skin cancer to add into the mix which was a timely reminder that I needed to pay attention to my thoughts, my health and what my body was trying to tell me. (NB: In the book "Metaphysical Anatomy" the author Evette Rose states the reason for skin cancer is when you *"try to be a part of life and fit into circumstances that do not resonate with you"*!).

I realised I was now suffering from Anxiety and was going through the Menopause too, but all the doctors could suggest was anti-depressants and sleeping tablets which I didn't want to take.

I knew then, on *that* morning, when I'd hit rock bottom, that nobody was coming to rescue me. This was down to me. And it felt like a huge mountain to climb, but at the same time strangely liberating.

So I did what I *had* to do, which was to take some form of action. I took one small step at a time and with each step forward, things started to change. Seemingly out of nowhere I was offered a good marketing position with a TV mini celebrity and although I still wanted my own business, I knew that I was on a path to somewhere......I just wasn't sure where. I was good at this role and after a couple of months I could feel my confidence slowly returning.

But the Universe wasn't done with me yet. Oh No....

The marketing agency went broke as the mini TV celebrity didn't know how to run a business and he had to let us all go, but the timing was perfect for what came next as it gave me the most precious time.

Because next came some *'Life events'*.

My beloved Father who had carried on heroically for 5 years after my Mum had passed away was now struggling to live in his own home anymore. We moved him to a beautiful care home where he lasted just a few months before he passed away at the grand age of 93 with both my sister and I at his bedside. With a mind and wit as sharp as anything until the last few days he was a huge loss in my life that I felt deeply.

I shared the grief with my lifelong best friend who had suffered from MS for the most part of her adult life, and I realised that she too had suddenly got worse and was now also fading away in front of my eyes.

The loss of my best friend happened just a few weeks later......

By now I was reeling from the grief and the shock of everything that had happened in just a few short months, but I knew......I just knew that my life was about to transform.

I felt very strongly that my Life's purpose was about to be revealed – there had been so much sadness that I knew it was time for some good and I made a decision to just *trust* that everything would be ok and I could feel myself surrendering to it and having faith.

The first good news came quickly – my skin cancer was gone and although they warned me it could come back anytime – I just knew it wouldn't and I can say that with 100% confidence. (And because there was NO way I was going to stay out of the sun for the rest of my life!).

Then I happened to be on social media scrolling my newsfeed and saw an advertisement for a woman who claimed to transform people's lives through a Therapy called Rapid Transformation Therapy (RTT) and that she could teach anyone to do it.

The woman's name (Marisa Peer) seemed vaguely familiar to me and I went back to check the audio meditation that someone had sent me that I had listened to on "that" morning. It was the same woman.

I looked at her Live Training program and it sparked the first real interest I had in anything for a very long while. What a great thing to be able to do – to help people to transform their lives and be free of limiting beliefs!

The live program was expensive and I wondered briefly how I would afford to do it, but once again, I just felt that I needed to trust my intuition and that somehow there would be a way – I just had no clue how, but I was starting to feel that my life was flowing in a direction that I couldn't control – but didn't want to either......it just felt right.

Then came the next piece of news – we had sold my Father's home in anticipation that he would need the funds for his care home – but with him being gone, there was just me and my sister.

The funds I needed for the program that came from the sale of the house came just a week before we buried my best friend and the very next day I arrived in London on a cold wintry and snowy day to start my training.

So here we are – 7 years after my life started to fall to pieces – and now I am an advanced RTT Therapist, (and one of their Trainers), a Clinical Hypnotherapist and a Success Mindset Coach with a thriving Practice running private and group Online Therapy programs transforming the lives of my clients. I truly LOVE what I do.

So what can I share with you today that I truly believe is life changing and that everyone should know, that helped me and helps my clients every day? Here goes....

A Useful Summary of the Power of our Mind!

- As humans, we are born believing we can do anything we set our mind to do, and we can achieve as much abundance and success in life as we want! We really CAN have a life of *"no limits"* if we understand how our mind works.

- Our brain is like a computer, and, like all computers, it has to have a base program to run off. Your base program is actually written and stored in your subconscious mind based on the thoughts and beliefs you created around 0-7 years old!! Just imagine what beliefs you might have created back then, about money, success, abundance? What was going on around you back then – what did you see and hear the most from your parents or main caregivers back then?

- After the age of 7 our subconscious mind effectively closes a big trap door and is no longer accessible during our normal waking hours. Your base programming is therefore done and is the blueprint for your life.

- It is **US** who create our upper limits and limiting beliefs based on those early childhood thoughts and beliefs. These early thoughts and beliefs will affect every aspect of our life and create our Identity which is stored deep in our subconscious mind. Our mind then ensures that our outer world is congruent with our beliefs and so we follow the same familiar patterns of behaviour that we've always done.

- Our subconscious mind is running our life for about 95% of our day.....from the program that we created in our childhood. If you're struggling to change something in your life – then it's because you hold a conflicting *thought* or *belief somewhere deep in your subconscious mind.*

- Fear. Fear is part of life, but fear will either hold you back or propel you forwards depending on how you look at it. When you hit a problem, how do you view it? If it's a road block then you have limiting beliefs around what you are capable of. If you see it as a hurdle that you need to learn from and then climb over or through it, then you are on the right track.

So how can we change our "programming" so that we can achieve success in ALL areas of our life?

1) It all starts with "Awareness". If you are operating from your subconscious mind for 95% of your day – then it's time to start paying attention to what your patterns are around the area that you want to change. Eg. for more success in your money journey, what are your patterns of behaviour around spending, saving, investing, etc so you can bring it into your conscious mind?

2) What is the upper limit that you have set on yourself and why? – Do you feel that you have an "upper limit" in a particular area of life? A good way of seeing this is to write on a piece of paper what you want, and then underneath write, "I can't have this because…

3) Notice what your limiting beliefs are and make a conscious decision to change by repetition of a new behaviour in order to change the programming! Hypnosis and Rapid Transformation Therapy is a much faster way to do this to help you to get to the root cause of WHY you have the patterns that you do and to replace them with better and more abundant thoughts.

4) Trust your intuition and your "feelings". Our body is actually 99.999999% ENERGY and only .0000001% solid matter!!! Our emotions are simply energy in motion and are there to guide us; all we have to do is feel them and notice them.

Let me leave you with a final tip – If you're reading this book, then the chances are you are looking to build wealth. But 80% of your wealth strategy is already determined by the stories you have told yourself over and over again that live deep inside your subconscious mind.

So no matter what investment strategy you use..... if you don't believe at a subconscious level that you will be wealthy.......then guess what? You won't be – your mind will make sure of it in order to 'protect' you.

Fix your subconscious beliefs FIRST, so that the strategies you learn will deliver your desired result and you will become unstoppable. (This goes for any part of your life too by the way....) – It's why one of my clients said to me about my "Passion, Purpose, Potential Program" – *"This should be the FIRST program anyone does in their business, not the last."*

5 Mindset Shifts that will Transform Your Life – https://MeButFree.com/5

CHAPTER 13

A Woman's TRUE Journey to Success and Wealth BEYOND STIGMA or STEREOTYPE

SAMANTHA HEARNE

Qualified business mentor, coach and CPD trainer

In this chapter we will be exploring the real reasons women:

- Hold themselves back
- Play small
- Dim their light
- Feel like they need to fit into a box
- When it comes to wealth, money, and your success

Think of it as a cathartic chapter focused on you, your next level and a real deep dive into how you can step things up in the most empowering ways! Strategy combined with magical reframes and a synergy with your energy and focus.

When it comes to a woman succeeding, you can tend to find this comes with many caveats or hidden agendas from others; do they have children, are they heartless, what have they sacrificed elsewhere, has a marriage broken down? The list of questions that would need to be answered before a woman is truly deemed to be 'successful in her own right' goes on. Rather than take the way she shows up and creates results to be enough, these caveats need justifying beforehand – why?

THAT is what I want to explore with you through this chapter and hopefully allow you to reach a point in your own embodiment, mindset and energy where YOUR success can come WITHOUT limits or fears and you can truly embrace the success you are destined for.

WHY?

Because as a woman, we need to showcase this more to the world. To those around us. To our network. The more you are able to create new levels of success, break moulds set by societal norms and create a new level of expansion – the more women, in every capacity, can start to really feel that anything is possible. Which it should be!

Creating a ripple effect of positivity and female empowerment is where we sit currently, where the focus for women in business lies, where the mission for women's success is championed.

So, knowing we are at this point in time where changing the narrative is being yearned for and there is a craving for female empowerment and success coming to the forefront of conversations, it seems fitting that this is our focus.

Personally, I have always gone against the 'norm'. Not in the conventional ways you may first think of; I went to university, I became a teacher, I bought a house, I got married – these things are very much societal norms, but where I went against the grain, is where I also realised how many women play small, get judged and feel like outcasts when you do decide to do things differently.

I left teaching to start an online business. I bought a house with my boyfriend after just 6 months together. I self-published a book in a week. I set up a YouTube channel with no experience and just my phone. I pivoted in business to align more with my big mission.

Again and again, I made bold decisions and acted. To me, this felt normal, natural, what I was made for. But this was always met with fear and concern; are you ready? Is this the best decision to make? Should you wait a little longer? What if it doesn't work? Are you sure?

Have you ever felt this resistance around you?

Felt restricted instead of empowered, when you choose to truly move and others see you doing it and present fear?

Felt guilty for striving for more?

Had a sense of shame around trying to create change or better yourself and the future because it just seems too big, bold or brave?

THIS – this is what we are transforming here together.

A woman's TRUE journey to success and wealth BEYOND STIGMA or STEREOTYPE

After making every bold decision I have, I continued to succeed, to reach new heights of my potential and to unlock new elevated versions of myself and this reinforced to me how much we live a life of two halves;

The one that we truly want to live, that lingers within us, in our thoughts and deep within our ambition.

The one we live to please others, to fit in and to keep things 'safe'.

Then there lives the 'in between'.

This space is where a brave woman DECIDES she no longer wants to leave her desires, biggest dreams and inner knowing hidden, to appease others or keep living a life others understand and start living the life she truly wants.

With all of this in mind, here are 3 top fears that come up for my clients and community when it comes to truly owning and creating their success (and I know they will come up for you too!)

1. What if people see me differently?
2. Will I have to become someone I don't want to be?
3. I feel like a fraud – other people are more successful than I am.

So let's unpick each one and get you to a place where success is no longer something you fear, self-sabotage or dull down – because you deserve more than that.

What if people see me differently?

Since when did being different become negative? Being different or seen as doing things differently becoming a problem?

If you want to achieve things you haven't achieved before, create success in ways you haven't created before – you will have to do things differently. You will have to create changes in your life, mindset and decision making in order to reach places you haven't reached yet.

In essence, being different, doing things differently, creating from a place of difference – is your only way to truly create a life of **success and wealth BEYOND STIGMA or STEREOTYPE.**

Because the longer you live within the safety lines of society or the expectations of others, the longer your success and wealth will come with restrictions.

So, the first big fear around being a woman that outrageously succeeds and builds wealth – she must and is always different!

Once you embrace this difference, those around you will also see things differently about you.

It will shift from:

Are you sure? TO wow, she is really going for it.

Why would she try and do things that way? TO I really need to be braver with my own decisions.

I think this is all too risky TO I wish I lived my life like she does. I am just so scared to do anything differently or make a change.

Again, you can see how the ripple effect takes shape when you realise that being different or seen to be doing things differently is NOT negative. It is needed.

It is needed for other women around you to realise that there never has to be any limits.

Will I have to become someone I don't want to be?

This narrative comes from movies, the media, online cultures; the women who succeed are selfish, greedy, tyrants, power hungry, neglect their family, heartless (we could go on!)

Some examples:

The devil wears Prada – Helen Mirren is portrayed as being cut throat, never around for her family, rude and obnoxious.

Erin Brockovich – wants to better herself and her family but is judged for having young children, wearing clothes less 'corporate', being a real person – would people take her seriously?

Hidden figures – the women behind the true magic and success, never acknowledged or mentioned.

At every turn a woman judged on her success VS her lifestyle and life choices.

Well – no more! And not for you.

You don't have to become someone you don't want to be. You have to become who you are MEANT to be. The version of yourself that is, the mum, the wife, the friend, the business woman, the WHOLE version of you.

The only reason women find themselves becoming someone they don't want to be, is when they become engulfed in what others think, want or decide for them and continue to play the people pleasing version of themselves, continue to live and follow the narrative that best suits rather than feels right and aligned.

I feel like a fraud – other people are more successful than I am.

Your journey and success is not about anyone else. It is about creating the life and future that best serves you, aligns with your big goals and visions, connects you to the way you want to live your life without limits – so feeling like a fraud is not what this is about.

It is about women constantly feeling like they have to compete with one another to 'reach the top' or 'make it'. Women feel like there is less space for them at the metaphorical success table and therefore the only way to get a seat is to take it from another woman.

What if – you start your own success table and make room for all the women doing the same and choosing the same as you? Success and wealth without stigma or stereotypes?

That way, this idea of 'not enough space for us all' 'she is more successful so must be better' dissipates.

It can become about the collective energy for women to rise up and build success without limits.

Wherever you are in your journey, if you created your own table – I guarantee you will have women wanting to join you there.

Feeling like a fraud is more about feeling like there is only one space for a successful woman in your 'genre' or 'niche' – so flip that and make it about embodying and embracing them all. All women can have a seat and when they do, the energy and success that builds will become so palpable, others around will be able to taste it and also want in!

So, although this chapter hasn't provided you with a formula to wealth or a 5 step process to more sales, cash and profit, I believe that this inner work and decision making up-levelling is key for you to be able to,

1. hold onto the success you build (as otherwise, when you achieve success, you can tend to self-sabotage and then go into 'hiding' for a period of time after)

2. embody your wealth and success without guilt or shame (this is key for the longevity of your success)

3. live fully into who you are meant to be (it starts with you, not the results you create, so believing and embodying yourself as

this next level version of wealth and success is where this all begins)

From here, I invite you to think about what you need to focus on to enable your success and wealth to come without shame or guilt and to continue to expand without a fear of the stereotypes that pre-existed your next level.

Money, success, wealth; are all energy, so let this work marinate within and become the inner work you fully commit to.

You deserve that, the women waiting to sit at your table deserve that, your future self deserves that.

If you resonate with this message and truly want to build (or sustain) a business with real profit but also on your terms, please reach out to & connect with Sam.

The entire ethos of Sam's work is to mentor women to wild success; in their income, profit, brand, community building & marketing with ease, ON THEIR TERMS. You never have to compromise on your goals or your life.

And if you're ready to upgrade your business in these 5 core areas – community growth, achieving your goals, marketing & messaging, sales & profit and organic lead generation – join Sam's 5 days of free mentoring inside the upgrade your business experience today.

https://www.samanthahearneproducts.com/upgrade-your-business-experience

CHAPTER 14

The Power of an Online Community

SAMANTHA POOLE

Founder of Ask GoTo & Incubation Nation CIC

In this chapter, I explain how my first Facebook group grew to 20,000 members without spending a penny, and how it has generated more than £250,000 in revenue over the last five years.

Along with highlighting the benefits of community management, monetizing, managing, and maintaining Facebook groups, I will also present some pitfalls.

How I grew My Group

It was back in 2010 when I was first drawn to Facebook Groups. As a new mother in a new area 13 years ago, there was no WhatsApp, so I had to send a single text message and wait patiently for a response. There are many emotions that come with being a new parent, and a supportive network can be extremely helpful in a variety of ways. As I worked full time in a police control room and did not have many friends outside of work, I found it difficult to find out about local groups, things to do, and finding new 'mum friends' back then.

It was a game changer for me to discover I could message all my new 'mum friends' in a Facebook group! I have been a fan of Facebook since day one, and I wouldn't be where I am without it! Using Facebook, I was able to maintain relationships with friends and family near and far, and I was able to share information with all my new 'Mum Friends' in one place. The group started with 20 mums and now has 21,500 members. It grows by 200/300 members a month mainly through word-of-mouth, and the group monitors every request for membership on a daily basis.

My group, **Mum to Mum Milton Keynes and beyond**, provides parents with a place to share their posts, get advice, and connect with other people who 'can help in that moment', because many parents do not have a safe space to talk to others 24/7. In online communities, many people share more openly than they do in person; perhaps because they can be anonymous and/or avoid the awkward nature of silence and stares. People want to feel like they belong, and online communities provide a space that makes people feel like they're part of something, even if it's just casual conversation.

To protect my members, I started posting anonymously for them so they could ask private questions. This may have taken extra time and at this point I was running the group for 'free' but I do feel it was an asset that has helped my group grow and secure its 'know, like, trust factor'.

I was delighted to see Facebook introduce anonymous posting as a feature in 2022!

It was back in 2017 when I experienced a difficult personal moment in a public place in Milton Keynes that I saw how well my group was working.

I was sitting in a restaurant trying to have a 'family meal' with my ex-husband and two kids who hate eating out due to sensory processing issues, especially if it's busy. I was left at the table alone, feeling stressed and upset when the waitress stopped to talk with me.

"Are you ok?" she asked

After explaining my situation briefly, she told me about this Facebook Group called Mum to Mum Milton Keynes, a wonderful online group that I should join. She told me about the amazing lady who runs the group and helps you post anonymously if you need support and guidance. In fact, she went so far as to get her phone out without her boss noticing to invite me to the group, and that was when I had to break the news...

With blushed cheeks and a little embarrassment, I replied, "I manage that group."

In response, she giggled and again commented on what an incredible resource it is for Milton Keynes parents. She went on to say that she tells all the mums who come into the restaurant about it since it is so helpful!

It was music to my ears, and it is the very way you want to expand your network.

At this point we only had about 2,000 members but it was great to hear that it was becoming known, liked and trusted. As a new mum in a new area it was hard to meet like-minded people but it looked like I had cracked this long before others started growing their online tribes. I had chosen from the beginning for it to be a 'private group' so when sharing we had an extra level of security, but that also meant that it would not be found like public groups could be found. It 100% relied on members inviting friends, and those friends inviting more friends. Friends have invited friends, 21,500 of them so far. Charities have been supported, and news articles have helped the group grow into a vibrant online community.

For those who are new to Facebook Groups, they are a place where a community can come together to engage on a shared interest, whether that's a cause, an issue or an activity. They're not the same as Facebook Pages, which were designed to be the official Facebook presence for any given entity (like a brand, business or celebrity). It's much better to be in a group, and I'll explain why in this chapter.

As with any organic marketing tactic, Facebook Groups don't just blossom overnight. You need to put the effort in to make your Group a success and give users a reason to sign up and stay! Believe it or not, I set this up purely to have all my new friends in one place but after a few years I was being paid as an influencer for sharing things we loved to do as a family. I was living my best life and making some money as a side hustle too!

Fact: Over 1.8 billion people use Facebook Groups each month, proving that millions turn to these more intimate online spaces in hopes of bonding with others.

Managing the Group

Daily interaction is key to keeping your Facebook group alive and growing. The admins of your group should keep the feed packed with regular and positive interaction and engagement. Don't be too lazy to like and comment on your members' posts regularly and make sure you answer most (if not all) of the questions they have about your service, product, or industry. Sharing other people's / businesses posts into the group is a great way to keep the group engaged; i.e. events, jobs, news and your partnerships' content too.

As we've grown, Rules or No Rules have become a big talking point! Rules aren't for the weak. It's your group, your time, your energy, your brand and your business in many ways. In my experience, three core components drive community growth: **Relevance, Relationships and Respect.**

- Communities can be complex to manage.
- Communities can be hard to build.
- **Communities require constant care and feeding.**

I think our group has been so successful because it has been managed well, it has grown organically and it has a strategy that supports both the members and the local businesses that work with us.

You should be clear about your reasons for starting a group before starting it, as maintaining a Facebook group requires a lot of effort. So make sure you're really invested in it and invest in some amazing admin assistants to help manage the group.

'People' are what make up Community Managers. During Covid-19, many groups provided assistance to their members in difficult times – furlough, financial hardship, loneliness and isolation, and bereavement. Messages will flood your inbox and DM's, so make sure you have support to make it successful! Some of us have a reason why we set up Facebook groups and what we want to accomplish, but many have started groups in the moment that have become a lifeline for the nation.

This group for example started as 'ideas to do in lockdown' with a handful of members and it now stands at 1.2 MILLION members:

FAMILY LOWDOWN TIPS & IDEAS – Private group – 1.2M members

Now they have a group this size they can monetise it! This group is now an asset and it has a loyal and engaged audience. This is definitely worth looking at if your product or service is suited to a national or international audience. Grow a generic group first and then you can create a 'niche' subgroup later.

The main benefit of having such a large organic group is that you manage what they see, what the banner is and what the members can post. Only businesses that work with me can 'advertise' in the group and display their business in the banner area.

My business grew to £85,000 in Year Three by letting local businesses advertise in my community, including creating a local magazine, selling a discount card in my Facebook group, and holding networking events.

Covid did affect this revenue in Year Four and I did have to pivot, but after five years this business is still growing and I am now looking to license or franchise my business model.

Monetising The Group

In 2010, when I launched Mum to Mum, I was not considering wealth or business, nor was I anticipating the popularity of Facebook groups for business. You must, however, have a strategy once your group becomes a way for others to profit from your efforts! It is not free to advertise in newspapers, on websites, and on banners that are seen by thousands of people, so why should it be free in your group?

This was the start of monetisation for me...

Starting a Facebook group is similar to starting a blog. You want to know who it's for, what you're going to provide in the group, and why you're starting one in the first place. Also, keep in mind that your members must have a specific need in common. Otherwise, you will struggle to find ways to create engagement with your members.

Value and kindness cannot be overstated, and it is crucial to manage trolls and approve posts or your community will quickly be damaged!

My idea was to help members find great days out, great offers, great businesses, jobs and a community of like-minded people to build friendships with. I learnt as I grew the group and it was not monetised until many years later.

It was a pleasant surprise to find that as the group grew I was offered a variety of opportunities, including free tickets to events, free days out, paid campaigns, and the opportunity to start my own business.

Among the ideas that generate money are:
- Brand Partnerships
- **Sponsored Posts**
- Start a business on the needs of your community – easily find gaps in the market from their questions
- **Connect buyers and sellers**
- Offline or online workshops – charge businesses who want to present in your group
- Paid courses – charge businesses who want to present in your group

- **Collaboration with experts, mumpreneurs, and local entrepreneurs**
- Bulk deals from companies – eg advertising tickets
- Offer your Facebook group banner as promotion space – eg £50 per week
- **Affiliate Marketing**

My 'hobby' and a place to connect with friends had evolved into a business, and I am forever thankful for this amazing opportunity.

I have learned a lot over the years and have experienced many highs and lows managing this group! Hopefully you'll find these hints and tips helpful if you're new to groups.

Creating Your Facebook Group Tips

To summarise, here are the five steps you should be following to take your Facebook Group from 0-20,000 members without spending a single penny:

1. **Decide on the who, what, and why of your group**

2. **Come up with a compelling theme for your Group – something that people will want to discuss and that you can offer genuine expertise on.**

3. **Decide who will manage the group and what value it will provide.**

4. **Set the rules and be clear on your reasons for these rules.**

5. **Promote your group and create the strategy to grow your group**

You will see your Group subscriber count rise when you follow these steps, iterate as needed, and keep track of it! Our online community brings people together and provides users with a quick and easy way to navigate and find a resolution to a problem.

The PRO'S and CON'S

Facebook groups may be hard to run, but they're great for your clients and for your relationship with them. If you set your group and strategy up correctly, they can also be an effective lead generation tool.

The Pro's:

1. **The ability to grow a group with millions of followers is sometimes quicker than on other platforms.**

2. By going live in the group, you can engage your audience on a more personal level.

3. **Engage in personal conversations with members and get valuable feedback.**

4. Promoting your brand or product can be quite effective and quite inexpensive.

5. **You can quickly reach your ideal customers through your group without paying for sponsored advertising because they are your ideal customers in a captive audience.**

6. Events can be created within your group and members can attend.

7. **Your content, brand, product, and service can be improved by gathering priceless insights.**

8. When your strategy works, you can make money from your group and grow successful partnerships.

9. **If you are targeting multiple social media platforms to grow your business, this keeps all your members in one place.**

10. As it grows and makes money, it becomes an asset when you wish to exit the business.

The Cons:

1. **Due to Facebook's third party nature, it is imperative that you keep email addresses for all members (where possible and GDPR compliant).**

2. Having a backup plan in case Facebook suddenly shuts down is vital.

3. **When others see the success of your group they can easily copy the name or content (this is the same though for most public content platforms).**

4. Facebook groups never sleep!

5. **Members will contact you 7 days a week – 365 days a year especially when they see you're online!**

6. One of the main disadvantages of Groups is that someone needs to constantly monitor membership requests, content and comments, because in a Facebook Group, members are always active, no matter what time it is. Failure to do so can result in the Group being reported for many different reasons.

7. **Depending on the Group's Privacy, posts need to be approved by Admins or Moderators before they can be published. When you have a large and active Group, this can be a very time-consuming process.**

8. Sometimes, large groups fail to adequately handle questions or comments, and things can turn negative. In order for a Group environment to remain safe for all members, admins and moderators must maintain a positive atmosphere.

9. **The power of publicity in a group is generally much lower, especially in a private or secret group.**

10. Groups won't show up on Google searches, whereas pages will.

After considering all this, I still believe businesses should utilise Facebook groups if they depend on a community for brand recognition and product sales.

Since 2010, social media groups have come a long way, and community momentum via B2C (business to consumer) and B2B (business to business) groups will invariably carry over into 2023. Local, global, physical, online, virtual, niche and mass communities will likely play an even more important part in all our lives.

Thanks for reading this chapter, and I'm honoured to have the opportunity to write alongside so many incredible women in business. Thank you, Kylie, for inviting me to be a part of this fantastic resource for women around the world!

Connect with Sam:

Instagram @samanthajpoole

LinkedIn – Samantha Poole

www.askgoto.com

www.incubation-nation.co.uk

CHAPTER 15

Make Your Personal Brand a Valuable Investment

SHARRON GOODYEAR
Personal Brand Photographer and Strategist

Why is it important to build your personal brand for your long-term wealth?

I want you to imagine that you are standing behind a glass wall, looking into a room filled with your ideal clients. You can see them, but they can only see themselves in the mirrored surface of the wall. All of these potential clients have the same problem, and you have the solution they need. However, they don't know you exist.

Now, imagine that you find a door and are able to walk into the room. You introduce yourself to some of the people in the room, but then quickly leave again. You repeat this process, dropping in and out periodically.

While you are in the room, you may be able to connect with a few of the potential clients, and they may even share their problem with you because they like you. However, because you are not present consistently, they have not had a chance to build up trust in you, which means they are less likely to invest in your solution.

Meanwhile, one of your competitors has been in the room the entire time. This person has spent a lot of time getting to know people and talking to them about how they can help. They have become known and liked in the room, and are being talked about by the others there.

Because they have consistently repeated their message and positioned themselves as the experts in their field, showing evidence of their work, they have also gained the trust of the potential clients. As a result, they are being recommended as the go-to person for this problem.

Now let me ask you, who in your opinion is winning in this situation?

I use the above analogy to illustrate the importance of building a strong and consistent personal brand if you want to establish long-term wealth. It also highlights the three key factors in attracting your ideal clients from your target audience: being known, being liked, and being trusted.

To be known, you must be present and actively engage with your potential clients. This means being visible and consistently sharing your message and expertise.

To be liked, you must establish a connection with your potential clients and build rapport with them. This involves showing genuine interest in their needs and concerns and being approachable and friendly.

To be trusted, you must consistently deliver on your promises and demonstrate your expertise. This requires building credibility and establishing a reputation as a reliable and trustworthy professional in your field.

By focusing on these three key factors, you can effectively attract your ideal clients and grow your business. It can also make it easier to form partnerships and collaborations with other businesses or individuals.

Having a strong personal brand can also help you cultivate a loyal following of individuals who are interested in your message and offerings. This can be particularly beneficial for building long-term wealth, as it can help you establish a sustainable business or career that is not solely dependent on your personal skills and expertise.

By building a loyal following, you can create a reliable source of support and income that can help you achieve financial stability and success over the long term.

What is the impact of building a personal brand?

Your personal brand can either significantly enhance your reputation and business success or damage it if not presented well. That is why it is crucial to build a strong personal brand that is based on your authentic values. This will ensure its effectiveness and success.

As previously mentioned, individuals are more likely to purchase from people and businesses that they know, like, and trust, and whose values align with their own. If your values are not evident in your actions or if there is a lack of consistency in your messaging, this can have a negative impact on your business.

It is important to ensure that your values are reflected in your practices and that your messaging is consistent in order to build trust and credibility with your customers and clients.

Developing a clear personal brand strategy and understanding the challenges and needs of your ideal clients is essential for creating the impact you desire in your industry. By clearly defining your personal brand and understanding the pain points of your target audience, you can effectively position yourself as a valuable solution and build trust with potential clients. This can be a key factor in achieving your goals and building a successful business or career.

There are also many potential benefits to building your personal brand. Here are a few potential impacts:

- Increased income: A strong personal brand can help you command higher fees for your products or services, as you will be perceived as an expert in your field.

- Greater opportunities: A well-known personal brand can open doors to exciting opportunities and collaborations, as you will be seen as someone who is respected and well-regarded in your industry.

- Improved credibility: A personal brand can help you establish yourself as an authority in your field, which can make people more likely to trust your expertise and advice.

- Enhanced reputation: Building a personal brand can help you build a positive reputation and be known for your skills, knowledge, and experience.

- Greater influence: A personal brand can give you a larger platform to share your ideas and message with a wider audience, which can help you make a bigger impact in your industry.

It's worth noting that these are just a few examples, and the specific impacts of building a personal brand will depend on your goals and the efforts you put into building and maintaining it.

While it's important for businesses to have a strong brand, it can also be beneficial for individuals within the business, especially business owners and leaders, to have a personal brand. Tim Cook, CEO of Apple has at the time of writing 13.9 million followers on Twitter. Apple itself has 8.9 million.

Richard Branson has 12.6 million Twitter followers compared to only 250k Virgin followers and Jeff Bezos has 6 million Twitter followers compared to 5.1 million Amazon followers. Which suggests that ultimately people love people more than they love brands!

This also demonstrates that your personal brand can really help you stand out as an individual and differentiate you from others in your industry. It can also help you establish yourself as an authority and thought leader in your field.

What Constitutes a Great Personal Brand?

A great personal brand is one that effectively showcases an individual's unique value proposition and establishes them as an authority in their field. A few key characteristics of a great personal brand include:

1. Clarity: A great personal brand is clear and concise. It clearly communicates the individual's expertise and what sets them apart from others in their field.

2. Consistency: A great personal brand is consistent across all channels. The individual's messaging, visual identity, and overall branding should be consistent across their website, social media, and other online platforms.

3. Authenticity: A great personal brand is authentic and genuine. It showcases the individual's true personality and expertise, rather than trying to be something they are not.

4. Relevance: A great personal brand is relevant to the individual's target audience. It addresses the needs and challenges of the audience and positions the individual as a valuable solution.

5. Differentiation: A great personal brand differentiates the individual from others in their field. It clearly communicates what sets the individual apart and why they are the best choice for their target audience.

By possessing these characteristics, a personal brand can be effective in attracting clients, customers, and opportunities and positioning the individual for long-term success.

How I Reinvented My Own Personal Brand

As a single mum to 3 children and one pooch, I work hard at juggling parenthood with managing a home and everything that comes with being a female entrepreneur. While it isn't always easy, I now have a very clear direction in terms of where I'm taking my business and also what I want from my life in general.

5 years ago however, things were very different. Having been a photographer for 12 years I was splitting my time between running a wedding photography business and maintaining a lifestyle blog called Keeping it Fabulous.

Although I was passionate about writing, working with brands and creating content, I wasn't able to sustain a living out of it. My enthusiasm for wedding photography after so many years was also starting to wane. I was starting to feel despondent and wanted change.

Needing some advice, I made a call to my photographer coach friend Gillian Devine. She gave me some simple yet life changing advice that would help reset the course of my business for the better.

"You need to work out what you enjoy, what you're good at and the types of people you want to work with. Write this down along with all your strengths and things you're passionate about and figure out how you make a business out of it."

Having followed Gillian's advice I was finally able to identify what I wanted my business to look like. I wanted to work with entrepreneurs and small business owners and elevate their personal brands through a mix of photography and personal brand strategy.

From this point, I had to reinvent my own personal brand, which included identifying my ideal client avatar, changing my messaging and creating a new website. Fortunately, I had also worked with business owners previously providing a headshot service, so was able to pull together a gallery to showcase my work as a personal branding photographer. I began networking to meet new clients and evolved my online portfolio as a result.

Whilst I was building my reputation as a personal branding photographer, I also spent a lot of time studying and learning about personal branding as a whole. I wanted to understand how the images I took could become part of my clients' overall strategy in terms of creating greater visibility for their brands.

During this time, I identified that there was actually a process that needed to be followed in order for my clients to maximise their visibility and attract the right people to their businesses. It was essential that they had their brand strategy in place first, followed by their visual branding.

By being clear on their values, ideal client, brand story, messaging and brand personality we could then design a shoot that embodied it all. This included, how they were styled, the location we shot in and the mood of the shoot from posing to expression and post production.

This led me to creating an all-encompassing service that meant they had real clarity on who they were as a personal brand and how they wanted to connect with their audience.

The framework I built and we do the deep work on, helps my clients get the results they want in their businesses faster and more efficiently as a result of following this process. I also now have a brand and business I love!

The Personal Branding Framework To Help Build Your Personal Brand

Whenever I work with a client on their personal brand, I start by understanding their values before everything. This is because our values act as the foundations from which our personal brand is built. In order to be truly authentic, we must make sure our messaging, brand story, brand personality and visual identity all align with our values.

1. Define your brand: Start by identifying your values, vision and mission. What is your unique value proposition and what sets you apart from others in your field? What are your strengths, skills, and expertise? What do you want to be known for?

2. Determine your target audience: Who are you trying to reach with your personal brand? What are their needs, challenges, and goals? Understanding your target audience will help you tailor your branding to meet their needs.

3. Your brand story: People are more likely to invest in you if they feel an emotional connection to your brand that aligns with how they see themselves or their values. Sharing your brand story helps build trust and loyalty in your audience.

4. Develop your brand messaging and establish your brand personality: Create a clear and consistent message that reflects your brand and resonates with your target audience. This should include your unique value proposition, your key messages, and your brand voice.

5. Create a visual identity: Develop a visual identity that reflects your brand and helps you stand out. This can include elements such as your logo, website design, and social media graphics.

6. Build your online presence: Establish a strong online presence by building a website and establishing a presence on social media platforms. Use these channels to share your message and engage with your audience.

7. Network and build relationships: Network with others in your field and build relationships with key influencers and potential clients. This can help you build your credibility and reach a wider audience.

8. Consistency is key: Consistently promote your brand and message across all channels. This will help you establish credibility and build trust with your audience.

By following this framework, you can effectively build a strong and successful personal brand.

How You Can Improve Your Personal Brand Today

1. Create high-quality visual content: Invest in high-quality images, graphics and video content to showcase your expertise and personality. This can help you stand out and build a stronger online presence.

2. Engage with your audience: Engage with your audience on social media and other online platforms. Respond to comments, answer questions, and share relevant content to build relationships and establish your credibility.

3. Share your expertise: Share your knowledge and expertise by writing articles, blog posts or creating videos. This can help you establish yourself as an authority in your field and build credibility with your audience.

4. Collaborate with others: Collaborate with others in your field or with complementary businesses. This can help you reach a wider audience and build relationships with key influencers.

5. Seek out speaking opportunities: Look for opportunities to speak at events or conferences or reach out to podcasters for

a potential guest slot. This can help you share your message with a larger audience and establish yourself as an expert in your field.

6. Create a professional-looking website with great photography. Invest in a professional-looking website that showcases your expertise and personality. This can be a key part of building a strong online presence and attracting potential clients or customers.

By implementing these strategies, you can continue to improve your personal brand and position yourself for long-term success.

My Wealth Investing Tip

Focus on building a strong and consistent personal brand as a way to attract long-term clients, investors or collaborative partners. A strong personal brand can help you differentiate yourself from others in your field and establish yourself as an authority and thought leader.

This can make you a more attractive option for potential clients, which can lead to increased income and long-term financial stability. By investing in your personal brand and consistently promoting it, you can create a sustainable source of income that can contribute to your overall wealth.

CHAPTER 16

Make Over £100K From Property Starting With Little Money

STEPHANIE TAYLOR & NICKY TAYLOR

Property Investors, Founders of HMO Heaven and
Rent 2 Rent Success.

Stephanie Taylor & Nicky Taylor are sassy sisters, property investors and Founders of HMO Heaven and Rent 2 Rent Success.

We spent decades believing that property and business success were not for 'people like us'. As Black women we didn't see many role models for property investing.

Property is a powerful tool for wealth building. Yet women don't invest in property at the same rate as men and on average women in the UK have a net wealth of £101,000 less than men (Office of National Statistics).

What we're going to talk about in this chapter is transformational. We'll show you how to start investing in property with little money, starting from exactly where you are.

In insider property circles it is known as rent to rent.

This is the strategy which helped us go from having no experience and little money to:

- Become property investors and developers with a multi-million pound property portfolio of blocks of flats, commercial property and HMOs.
- Start an award-winning property management company, HMO Heaven.
- Create Rent 2 Rent Success to help thousands of non-traditional investors get started in property.
- Write the #1 best-selling book Rent 2 Rent Success.
- Launch the top 1.5% podcast of the same name.
- Win Inspirational Person of the Year 2021
- Being featured on The BBC, and in The Telegraph, Business Insider and many others
- Setting up an accommodation and education trust to help people who struggle to find beautiful affordable homes.

We're passionate advocates that ethical property investment is available to anyone who wants it. And we're especially keen to inspire more women and women of colour to get started.

Perhaps you've always been interested in property but because you aren't in a position to buy a property right now, you've dismissed it.

I felt the same way for decades. And I'd never have had the courage to try if it wasn't for an everyday telephone which changed everything.

My mum telephoned me.

Mum was ill. She tried to sound upbeat, but I could hear that she was scared. I feel so ashamed. Yes, I was worried about Mum, but I was also worried about work and the project meeting, and the presentation, and… And other things that seemed so important at the time.

That was the day something changed for me. As I sat at my desk that afternoon, it hit me like a punch in the belly. My mum was scared and alone in Birmingham and I still went to work in Bristol. I should have been with my mum.

It came to me with clarity that day that the bank would be absolutely fine without me, but my mum wouldn't.

I'll bet there are very few people who, on their death beds, wish they'd spent more time working. And there are countless millions of people all over the world who wish they'd realised sooner how to create the freedom to give themselves more time with their loved ones.

That day, I made making the leap a must, and I finally committed to feeling the fear and doing it anyway.

What exactly would I do though? With so many failures to look back on, would a business really work for me without any experience? I wondered what I could do, and it came to me: property! It seemed an easier type of business to understand.

I started investigating property strategies and was blown away to learn that there are ways to get started in property with little money.

Initially I was sceptical though, rent to rent sounded too good to be true. And some property 'trainers' have a sleazy approach which is off-putting.

Because you're reading this book, I know that creating wealth ethically is important to you too; we decided to focus on running our business with care and making it a win-win-win for owners, for housemates and for us.

So what is rent to rent?

Most people have heard of buy to let where you buy a property and rent it out. Even for less expensive properties, you're likely to need over £50,000 to cover the deposit, buying costs and refurbishment. And you'd typically make between £200 and £400 per month after costs. Therefore, you'd need a lot of money to replace your salary.

The basis of rent to rent is that you rent a property from the owner and rent it out again. This means you don't need £50,000, and you make between £500 and over £1,000 per month per property after all the costs.

We truly love the elegant simplicity of this business model.

- You rent a property, usually for 3-5 years.
- You pay the owner a guaranteed rent, and usually you take on paying the bills.
- You rent the property out to tenants for a higher rent than you're paying the owner.
- The difference between the rent you receive from tenants and the rent you pay the owner, after the property running costs, is the profit that you make for your business.

It's an incredibly efficient business model, because it:

- Requires little money to start up.
- Means you can be profitable within a few months.
- Gives you consistent recurring cashflow.
- Gives you the names and addresses of your perfect customers.

We focus on HMOs (houses in multiple occupancy). An HMO is what you may know as a student house share, where each housemate has their own bedroom and then shares a kitchen and bathroom, although some HMOs may have ensuites or individual kitchenettes.

Let's compare a property being let out to a family with a property being let out as an HMO, by the room.

A two-reception, four-bedroom single let property, could rent to a family for £1,000 per month.

The same property as a five-bedroom HMO (using one of the reception rooms as a bedroom) could rent for £600 per month per room. This is equivalent to £3,000 for the property. Although you would usually be paying the bills in an HMO, the cashflow is significantly higher from an HMO than a single let, even after the bills.

Well that sounds great but the next question people often ask is…

… Is it legal?

Yes, rent to rent is legal.

Many people just can't believe that rent to rent is a legitimate business model because you can make a significant amount of money and get started with little money.

When I first came across it, I thought: 'surely it's not legal', and 'why have I never heard of it before?!'

Rent to rent has been used in commercial property for a long time. Commercial leases are leases that give a commercial property tenant the right to sublet a property.

This model came over into residential property and has been adapted to give residential landlords similar guarantees to the ones that commercial landlords enjoy.

The reason why some people think rent to rent might be illegal is that subletting usually comes to public attention when it's in the news because someone has done it illegally without the knowledge of the property owner. That is absolutely not what we advocate.

Rent to rent is legal when it's done with the full consent of the owner with the right contracts in place. Rent to rent is recognised by the UK government's Property Ombudsman, the Property Redress Scheme.

Will it work in a recession?

In a recession demand for rental properties increases.

Spareroom is the UK's biggest website for renting HMO rooms and its statistics show that rental demand is at its highest rate in over 10 years.

In recessions:
- Rental demand goes up.
- Rents go up.

- More landlords want guaranteed rent.
- Risk goes down.

So, although people think that getting into rental in a recession is bad, they are wrong. Even in a market downturn, people need somewhere to live. And people love that HMOs provide an easy 'all bills included' option. We're experiencing higher demand than ever.

Now is a great time to get started.

What about high utility bills?

The economic context we operate in is something we can't control but how we respond to it is something we can. There are businesses that thrive in both recessionary times and boom times. Our model of rent to rent is like that.

These are the steps we take to ensure that we still have a profitable business even if utility bills get higher.

- Analyse our properties using the Rent 2 Rent Success Deal Analyser.
- Use a smart automated heating control in the properties.
- Include a cap on utility spend in the contracts with owners.

The opportunity that higher utility costs bring is that more landlords are open to working with rent to rent businesses now.

It's a great time to get started.

Here's a real-life example of how it works in practice.

Loise Wilson's story

"For over 20 years, I dreamed of getting into the property business. But as a busy working mum with a successful career as a corporate accountant, it was always on the back burner and it didn't ever seem like the right time to start.

Property just didn't seem accessible to someone like me, and it was very rare to see females in property.

I think what really gave me the confidence to try property was when I was asked to run a charity food bank for our church. The food bank became a greater success than I could have imagined. I realised that if

I could make a success of the food bank, then I could start in property too.

With this in mind and a new-found confidence, My Cosy Homes was born, and I am so glad that my dream is now my full-time reality."

Loise found her first property in Croydon, London. It was in good condition, so she spent very little getting the property ready.

Now Loise is making over £1,400 per month after all costs on her first property.

And that's just the beginning…

Why 5 is the magic number

As every parent knows, five years go very quickly and a lot can change in that time. When we compare a baby with a five-year-old we can see the incredible growth that takes place in five years.

It's the same in property. Take the steps and, within a few months your life will change a bit. Within five years, it will change a lot. And that is where the magic happens.

Let's take Loise's first property as an example.

Profit after costs:

- Every month £715
- Every year £8,580
- Every five years £42,900

That's amazing, isn't it? For a few hours work each month, Loise earns a significant extra income after all the costs have been taken out.

So the question is: can you imagine how amazing it would feel to have your first property?

Imagine telling your family, friends, and colleagues, all the doubters, that it really does work. How would it change your life if you had an extra £42,000 of income over the next five years?

And even very few properties can be life-changing.

With just three properties like Loise's first one, you would have £2,145 cashflow per month. That is £25,740 per year, which for some people is a full-time UK salary. Incredibly, the cashflow on three average properties adds up to £128,700 over five years.

That's the life-changing power of rent to rent.

And it doesn't end there, you can use the money you make from your rent to rent properties to invest in buying your own properties. Rent to rent can be a first step to building a property portfolio that you own as we have done.

Are you in?

Next step

If you are interested in finding out more about how rent to rent can help you get started, we'd love to send you a free copy of our book Rent 2 Rent Success. It includes our 6 step system for success.

https://rent2rentsuccess.com/iconic

Our wealth tip

Your future is created by the actions you take today. It's something we often forget in the moment.

Most people use their income to pay their bills and don't have savings or investments. As they get older they will need to continue to work or rely on income from the government or other sources.

These 3 simple steps will ensure that you enjoy your life and have the funds you need for freedom.

1. Save
2. Invest
3. Enjoy, envision and give

Save

Saving requires being intentional about your money. Make yourself, your family and your future the first 'bill' you pay. Save first. You wouldn't miss your mortgage or rent, don't miss paying yourself. Save first. If you save 'what's left after bills' you'll do what most people do and save nothing. Even if you have to start with £10, £1 or even 10p. Start saving.

Invest

Once you have a little money saved, you're ready to start investing in assets. An asset is something you buy which makes you money. You need to own assets which make you money so that at some point in the future you're able to live on the income from your assets and choose whether to work.

We love the asset of property. It gives you cashflow each month and when you own property it also goes up in value over the long-term. If you're not ready to buy property yet, you can start in rent to rent as we've discussed in this chapter. Or other asset classes might suit you better.

The key thing is to invest and have your money working hard for you rather than the other way around.

Enjoy, envision and give

Many people find saving and investing boring or difficult to do. That's one of the reasons so few people do it. However, when you enjoy the money you have now and envision the future you want to create for yourself, it becomes fun.

Each month allow yourself an amount for fun and enjoyment. At first this might be small, but it'll grow over time. Make sure you only spend this money on indulgences and fun experiences.

With every month's payment to saving or investing you are giving yourself the gift of the exact life you want to create for your future. Take time to envision the future you want for yourself. Maybe it's to retire earlier. Maybe it's to have 'mini-retirements' every year. Maybe it's to travel the world. Whatever it is, you give yourself the gift of freedom to choose when you invest.

Finally, give.

Give before you're ready. I used to think I'd need to wait until we hit a certain revenue target or income. Then I heard about the 1% Pledge.

You could give 1% of your income, or revenue or whatever you choose. The beauty of the 1% Pledge is that it feels possible. Today.

Giving is a joy; it's such a privilege to be in the position to be a giver. It makes your heart sing. It makes your step spring. When you give, you're doing what we're all here to do: you're making the world a better place.

It's a great feeling to know that, as we do our work, we're having a positive impact on others. We believe we're all here to leave our world better, and each of us does this in a different way.

We are hugely grateful to have learned what is possible and had the courage to start.

I hope you have the courage to take action on your dreams too.

CHAPTER 17

Mix It up Baby

VIX MUNRO

Money & Wealth Coach

Most people have the potential to become wealthy, though some people have it a lot easier than others. Sure, your background is important but your drive, curiosity, and desire to improve yourself are more important. Which means it's less about where you've come from, and more about where you're going.

I don't come from a rich family, nor did I marry a rich man. And I've been able to create and build wealth so that I can live my life my way. I'm now a multi-millionaire. But don't get me wrong – I'm not denying my privilege. I'm white, cisgender, university educated and born in a first world country. And that helps.

The thing about wealth is that it means different things to different people. There's no rule that says you have to have a net worth of £1 million to be considered wealthy. Some people need less money to feel wealthy and others need more. Ultimately, wealth is a feeling, not a number.

The other thing about wealth is that there are multiple ways to acquire it. Most people have built wealth over the long-term, just done it in different ways. Very few people have inherited wealth and even less have achieved wealth through winning the lottery.

I didn't build my wealth the conventional way as I've invested a lot in non-traditional (or alternative) assets. But this doesn't mean that I ignore traditional assets altogether, as I still include traditional assets in my portfolio.

I now help women create and grow wealth too. I want to see a world with more wealthy women. A society where more women are financially secure is a society that benefits everyone. When women have money, we're able to make our own choices, invest in ourselves and our communities, and create a more equitable future for all.

I started my own wealth journey in property. I'd dabbled a bit before then, but it was buying my first investment property in 1998, that really got me started. Very few people were investing in real estate then. Instead, people were still recovering from the effects of the house price crash of the early 1990s. But I'd recently read Robert Kiyosaki's 'Rich Dad, Poor Dad', which had been published the year before, which inspired me. And buy-to-let mortgages had recently become available in the UK, which made it possible.

Initially, I focused my investment efforts on real estate as I was convinced that this was the best way to grow wealth. But as time went on, I realised that I was putting all of my eggs in one basket and didn't want to be hit hard in the event of a housing market crash.

So, I started diversifying my portfolio. I already had a workplace pension and became much more involved in what it was invested in. I also began to look for other opportunities.

I later diversified my portfolio further by investing in commodities, particularly precious metals. They have been a store of value for centuries, and have consistently maintained their value over time, which makes them a good hedge against inflation and market volatility.

I started investing in cryptocurrencies in 2017. I was initially drawn to the decentralised nature of cryptocurrency and the potential for high returns. It's been a rollercoaster ride, with lots of ups and downs, as the market is highly volatile. But I believe strongly in the long-term potential of the cryptocurrency market, so I see it as a very valuable addition to my portfolio.

I started investing in start-ups in 2018. I liked the idea of being in at the beginning. I mean, who doesn't wish they'd invested in Facebook or Amazon in the early days? I was also attracted by the tax benefits. Whilst it's risky, I mitigate the risk by investing in multiple start-ups rather than putting all my eggs in one basket with a single start-up. This has given me exposure to innovative areas, like medical/recreational cannabis, artificial intelligence, cyber security, ocean conservation and recycling.

There's risk associated with investing, whatever you invest in. However, this is considered to be much higher for alternative assets than it is for traditional assets.

Traditional investments are generally considered to be cash, publicly traded stocks, and bonds. And non-traditional or alternative investments are considered to be everything else – like real estate, hedge funds, private equity, precious metals, commodities, collectibles and cryptocurrencies.

The concept of traditional investments is that they're well-known assets, so what the typical investor would think about with respect to investing. And as many more people are investing in real estate, some people now consider real estate to be a traditional investment too.

Other alternative investments are becoming more mainstream now too. In particular, more and more people are adding gold and silver to their portfolio, often because they're considered safer than other assets, particularly during uncertain economic times.

My allocation to alternative assets is higher than that of your average investor. I have a high tolerance to risk, and I believe it's a great way to diversify my portfolio and increase my potential for returns. I'm also an early adopter. It was my early investments in real estate, when few were doing it, that then increased in value over time, and enabled me to become a millionaire.

I also invest for the long-term, which is essential for growing wealth. There are some exceptions which I'm intentional about.

Many personal finance experts focus mainly on traditional assets and don't cover the full range of alternative assets available. And if that works for them and you, that's great. I talk about investing in both traditional AND alternative assets because that's what I do myself. As an entrepreneur, I like to think outside the box. And as an investor, I like to invest outside the box too.

There are multiple ways to acquire wealth. Many people are happy with a traditional approach, investing primarily in stocks and bonds, with some, albeit limited, exposure to alternative assets.

Other people focus on a single asset class, with limited exposure to other asset classes. I see this a lot with property investors. They believe that property is the best investment – it provides income, capital appreciation, and is accessible to the masses.

But I increasingly see women who want to do things differently. They've often already started a business to provide them the lifestyle they want. And know that they need to put other things in place in order to build wealth over the long term. But it all feels too traditional for them.

So, either they haven't started investing because they don't know how to start and make it exciting and fun at the same time. Or they have started but don't feel that it's aligned to them and their goals.

They often also want higher returns and have a higher tolerance for risk. Entrepreneurs are generally more open to risk than the average person. In starting a business, entrepreneurs take a risk in order to achieve their goals, often finding the risk exciting. And that higher tolerance for risk usually extends into investing too.

It can feel lonely being a woman with a high-risk tolerance. Traditionally women are more interested in saving than investing. And women tend to be more risk-averse than men and thus more conservative as investors. Add to that that many personal finance experts don't talk directly to you, so it's no surprise that you feel alone.

But you're not alone. Increasingly, women are telling me that they want to take a higher risk for a potentially higher return and invest more in alternative assets. And that they're concerned that many opportunities only seem to be available to wealthy people and they want in too.

For years, many financial advisors have recommended a traditional allocation of 60% to stocks and 40% to bonds. Many still advocate this. Others now believe that a more diversified portfolio is a better strategy. However, the extent of diversification is still very limited with many financial advisors (i) recommending a very small allocation to alternative investments; and/or (ii) prioritising some alternative assets over others e.g., gold, silver and real estate.

Many personal finance experts don't talk about all alternative investments, particularly cryptocurrencies and private equity. This could be because they don't invest in these themselves, they believe they're too risky, or they're restricted from talking about them due to regulations in their country. This can be alienating if these feel exciting to you.

Investing in alternative assets offers an opportunity to diversify an investment portfolio and introduce more interesting and exciting elements of risk. Alternative investments can be more volatile but also offer potentially higher returns. They also provide a way to tap into different sectors or industries that may be unexplored or difficult to access. And offer a way to invest in something that is personally enjoyable or meaningful.

Alternative investments are not suited for everyone as they require a high tolerance for risk and may require your capital to be tied up for long periods of time. But they can be a great way to add variety and excitement to your portfolio. They're not right for everyone. So, you need to consider if it's the right fit for you.

If you want to diversify your investment portfolio by investing more in alternative assets, then here's a framework for getting started.

1. Assess your tolerance to risk

The first step is to assess your tolerance to risk. Alternative investments are usually higher risk than traditional investments, so it's important to understand how much risk you're comfortable taking on. This will be dependent on your investment goals, the time you have to achieve your goals, and the amount of money you're willing to lose.

2. Decide how much of your portfolio to allocate to alternative investments

The next step is to decide how much of your portfolio to allocate to alternative investments. This will depend on your risk profile. Even people with a low risk-tolerance will likely have some alternative assets in their portfolio. If you're someone with a high tolerance to risk, then your allocation will be a lot higher.

3. Decide what alternative assets to invest in

Before you start investing in alternative assets, it's important to understand the options available, how they work, and the potential risks and rewards for the different alternative assets. And then decide which ones you want to invest in. If you want really broad diversification, then you might decide to invest in all of them. Again, your decision will be dependent on your risk profile, investment goals and the time you have to achieve your goals.

4. Decide on your allocation to different alternative assets

Next, decide how much of your portfolio to allocate to each alternative asset. This will depend on your financial goals. For example, if you're looking for steady income, then you might want to allocate more to real estate. Alternatively, if you're wanting more growth, then start-ups may be more suitable. Remember that diversification is key to any investment strategy as that spreads risk, and alternative investments are no exception.

5. Decide on the investments you want to make within each alternative asset class

You likely won't be making these decisions immediately and you may also need to wait for the right opportunities to present. So, it's more about having a plan about what you want to invest in. For example, with real estate, do you want to invest yourself (in residential, holiday or commercial property) or gain exposure to real estate through a real estate investment trust (REIT)? There may also be tax benefits that you want to take advantage of.

6. Get support

You may want to engage a personal finance expert to help you with this. This could be a financial coach, mentor, educator, or financial advisor – depending on what kind of support you want. Usually, only a financial advisor can give you financial advice. But if you want coaching, guiding, educating, or mentoring, then there are other options open to you. And not all personal finance experts are created equal. Some may have more expertise and experience than others, particularly with respect to alternative investments, and some may be more suited to your needs than others. It's important to find someone that you feel will work well with you.

7. Regularly review and rebalance your portfolio

It's important to regularly review your portfolio to ensure it's still aligned with your goals, risk profile, so that you can make any necessary adjustments. It's also important to review your investment goals and risk profile on a regular basis to reflect any changes in your financial situation or personal circumstances. This may mean you need to change your allocation to alternative assets or select different alternative assets. With some alternative assets, this can be done immediately. But others are illiquid so rebalancing your portfolio will need to reflect this and may also need to happen over time.

Sometimes, it can feel overwhelming to get started. So, if you know you want to invest in alternative assets, but you know little about them, then start by researching and educating yourself about the different types of alternative assets available. You can do this by reading articles and books; attending webinars, seminars and courses; and joining online communities or forums where investors share their knowledge and experience with alternative investments. This will help decide which alternative assets align best with your financial goals, risk tolerance and time horizon.

Alternatively, you can get started immediately. If you're going to do this, then I suggest starting small. This will allow you to get a feel for the different types of alternative investments and how they perform, without having to risk a large amount of money. Some alternative investments are illiquid, like real estate, so you won't be able to do that immediately, though you can start looking for opportunities.

Here's some examples of things you can do immediately:

- invest in a REIT (Real Estate Investment Trust);

- invest in an exchange traded fund of physical gold or silver;

- buy gold and/or silver coins/bars;

- buy cryptocurrencies (the most common of which are bitcoin and ethereum);

- invest in a start-up through a crowdfunding platform, like Seedrs or Kickstarter.

And lastly, I want to remind you that building wealth takes time and patience, as well as having a solid plan. You're not going to become wealthy overnight. We're talking about building sustainable wealth and that's a long game. Nor will you get wealthy by accident. So, don't let the fear of the unknown or the fear of being overwhelmed stop you from achieving your financial goals. Remember that small steps can lead to big outcomes. So, create a plan and take action towards that plan every day.

It's your time. Are you ready?

Vix Munro is an economist, entrepreneur, author, money enthusiast and eternal optimist. She's passionate about helping women create and build wealth so that they can live the lives they want.

CHAPTER 18

Multiple Income Streams

WENDY WHITTAKER-LARGE

Dynamic HMO Investor, Coach & Author

"Money is only a tool. It will take you wherever you wish, but it will not replace you as the driver."
— Ayn Rand, novelist and philosopher

If you've watched any one of the plethora of TV property programmes you'll know the draw of owning property, and especially the draw of owning property that brings you income week in, week out. Perhaps you hold a secret yearning to be one of those people who can spot a deal, come up with the cash, and a few weeks later be making amazing profits from your newly renovated two-up two down. You rinse and repeat this again and again, and within a couple of years you can leave your job, sail round the world on your super yacht and watch with disdain for those who are still in the rat race.

Looks enticing doesn't it? And that's because it is.

The thought of 'passive' income – or income that is a result of money working for you and not you having to go out and slog for another £2 per hour in your pay packet, is a VERY enticing idea. It's what makes people cash in their savings, borrow huge amounts of money, and start talking about the first fix and second fix with utter confidence.

The truth is though, that investing in property is not a get rich quick game. It takes time, effort and plenty of hard work. It challenges your notions of money, of your own identity, and of what you think is possible in life. Investing takes you out of your comfort zone and pushes you to grow to be a better business woman, a better investor and a better human being. I can honestly say that investing in property changed my life – but it took time, money (that I didn't always have) and commitment.

The property investing world has generally been a man's domain until very recently. Although women had varying degrees of property rights and financial freedoms throughout history, it was technically legal for banks to refuse loans and credit to unmarried women (or require a husband's permission for married applicants) until the Equal Credit Opportunity Act was passed in 1974. The world of property and finance has been mostly male-dominated throughout history, but all that is changing now! There are more and more women realising that their future wealth and well-being cannot depend on a man. They are also realising that they need to take charge of their finances, educate themselves about investing, and create alternative income streams.

Today, women are asserting their skills in the property industry, which have up to now been undervalued and overlooked. Skills and innate talents that they are using to influence and enable the property world to evolve. Aspects such as an ability to see the bigger picture, an appreciation of aesthetics and design, a skill in analysing risks v rewards, an understanding of the practicalities of a plan, and a recognition of the human elements of renting and selling.

These are typically female traits which women are less scared to use in their drive to create wealth for themselves. Whether it is through great design, amazing service provision for tenants, bigger picture thinking towards growth, or simply superb customer service – we are changing the world of property and benefiting from it ourselves.

If you are reading this thinking that you know nothing about construction and can't stand the thought of all that dust and bricks and mortar, then never fear! It's not all building sites and hard hats. Yes there will be some of that, and if you plan to add value to property in any significant way, there will be plenty of building and renovating work to oversee. The good news is that you can learn it. You don't need to know how to rewire a house before undertaking a refurb project – you don't even need to know how to rewire a plug (that was about the level I was at when I started). Most builders are happy to explain in their own unique way how a construction project works, and although you may be baffled by some aspects, generally most projects have a similar process and schedule. Once you've done a couple of refurb projects, you'll be able to talk about stud walls, RSJs and fire boarding with the best of them.

The current property investing world is wide and varied. Unlike twenty years ago when I started, there are courses everywhere on every strategy you can imagine. Some of these include buy to let (BTL), Buy-Refurbish-Refinance (BRR); flipping (refurbishing a property and selling it for profit); Serviced Accommodation (holiday lets); Rent to Rent (R2R); Rent to SA; Commercial Conversions, title splitting; developing land; commercial property investing, and my own personal favourite – Houses of Multiple Occupation (HMOs).

All of these strategies use different tools of the trade to create income and wealth. Some are repeatable short-term strategies where you receive income through capital chunks (like flipping), whilst others are intended to create a portfolio from which you draw income each month (HMOs and BTLs). In all cases, the key is to add value.

If you can add value to a property or land – whether that is via capital uplift, alteration of use, extending/developing/adding value through planning permission, refurbishing or renovating – this is how you make money from property.

Why HMOs?

When I was in my twenties, I was a typical at-home mother of two young boys. Constantly pulled from pillar to post trying to do far too much in far too little time. Watching my other friends with envy who seemed to be spectacular super-mums to their children, and sexy superstars to their husbands.

When I looked in the mirror in the morning, rather than a vixen all I saw was a rather harassed looking badger, and all too often I would find party invitations or important school letters weeks after the event buried in the bottom of my handbag, slightly tinged with coffee stains or covered in crumbs.

Ah well, with my alternative cleaning methods, my boys would get more than their fair share of antibodies from the environment – they wouldn't need vaccinations to protect them from harmful viruses.

One of the reasons I was under pressure was not just having two children under the age of three. It was also due to juggling a part-time job, helping out at church, being on the pre-school committee, doing up our own home, being cook, cleaner and housekeeper and managing it all on a very tight budget. My husband was a teacher, which although sounds positive, he had only just finished training when we had also recently moved house (more children = more rooms needed). He was still on the first rungs of his career, yet we had a bigger mortgage and more outgoings to meet. There were times when we had plenty more month than money.

Life was hard and I could only dream of having more. The stress caused by having just enough money (yes just enough but no more) was immense. Raising a family and also having aspirations for a better life tugged at my heartstrings as I wanted to give my family a wonderful home life and to be there for them – not worrying about money or making ends meet constantly.

But within just a few short years, I had created a small portfolio of properties that gave me an additional income stream and enabled me to give up my job, have some much needed home help, and take back my time. With (by then) another two boys in the family mix, this was vital. I was pretty good at producing babies but by the time the fourth was born I decided to call it quits!

What I had realised was that turning a house into a cash machine was the way to make the most amount of money from the least amount of money. Instead of renting a house to one family, I could take exactly the same property but give it a refurb and rent the rooms individually. This allowed me to make significant profits each and every time. After the first HMO was completed, I already felt a weight lifted from my shoulders.

The impact of another £1000 coming into the family bank account per month, was, for me, huge. I felt like I could breathe again. The end-of-month rush to move money around from savings account to current account to make sure there was enough to pay the mortgage was no more. Or realising that the car insurance needed to be renewed in two months' time, at the same time as paying a deposit on a much-needed holiday (usually a caravan in Wales) was before, a real pressure – now, we could do both.

The strategy that made the most impact on my income and my bottom line was HMOs – Houses of Multiple Occupation: where you take an ordinary property and rent out the individual rooms to tenants. Usually, a property is rented to a family or a couple – and this can make you money if you do it enough times.

But imagine that on steroids! That's what an HMO does – it multiplies your income exponentially and if you have set it up correctly it can do this month after month after month. Generally you will take care of the bills so that the tenant pays a flat fee for his or her rent. It is straightforward for them, flexible and attractive, and it allows you to create multiple streams of income in just one property. The other benefit of investing in HMOs, is that you can recycle your initial pot of money and start all over again with another property once the first is done.

Imagine having 5 HMOs all making around £1000 per month profit. What would that do for you?

That's exactly where I was in 2013 and over the next three years I built a business that gave me financial freedom from the rat race and never having to worry about money again.

What's holding you back?

In my experience of working with people who want to get started in HMOs there are three areas that hold them back -

- Time
- Money
- Knowledge

HMOs are a highly lucrative and addictive strategy – once you've got a house making you £1000 profit per month, who wouldn't want another one? But the problem is without the correct knowledge, you could set yourself up for problems. There is specific legislation and rules that you must follow. You need to know about licensing and tenancies and housing law. All of this takes time to learn and implement. One of the best ways you can learn about HMOs is by reading, listening and learning from other people who have created profitable property portfolios. As they share their stories you will glean information and understanding about the ins and outs of HMOs. I also believe that mentoring and training is vital to help you achieve your goals. Unless we're being held accountable and have an actionable plan, most of us fail to achieve our dreams, as we often need a more experienced person hand-holding and staying one step ahead to guide, correct and challenge us.

One of the most liberating aspects of property investing is that anyone can do it. You don't need any special qualifications or skills, you can learn this, no matter what standard of traditional education you reached. I have known many women who had fairly average jobs or careers become massively successful property investors. All it takes is passion, commitment and a decision to make it happen.

You will also need some money to get started. You can pursue a strategy called Rent to Rent where you rent a house and turn it into an HMO. This is a very profitable strategy if you can find a good deal and use the cashflow to build up a pot of capital. Personally I prefer the approach of ownership – where the property is under my ultimate control which is why I always try to secure them through ownership or lease options (another more advanced strategy).

HMOs are a powerful strategy because they create enough cashflow for you to be 'investable' – that is, you can use other people's money to buy, refurbish and refinance a property, without using any of your own money. This was especially important to me, as I ran out of all my money after my second HMO and had to learn quickly how to use OPM (Other People's Money). HMOs are an ideal strategy for this as there are plenty of profits to share. If you have little time you might also be thinking 'I can't do this' but with a simple system, it all becomes much easier. In fact, whenever I have tried to take on a big challenge in life (and believe me, if your goal is to be financially free, then this is a big challenge) I've learnt that it's always much easier to break it down step by step.

How you use your time is the big question we all face day to day and month to month.

Whether sitting in front of the TV, going to the gym or having a pint at the local pub is how you spend your leisure time, now you will also have to fit in learning about and doing property. This is an investment into your future though. This is something you will always have and can always use. It can lead to a manageable portfolio that gives you a very comfortable second income – or you can grow a multi-million pound property investment company, the choice is yours!

You will find the time if this goal is important to you, and once you have achieved the ability to say goodbye to your job through all that lovely residual HMO income, your time will increase massively.

A Five-Step System

After developing three HMOs it dawned on me how tangled up the process can be to create an HMO – and even I got lost sometimes in the busyness of buying, refurbishing and tenanting. Making sure that everything was done correctly and compliantly was really important to me, but how could I be sure not to miss anything?

I decided to write out my methodology and what emerged was a simple 5 Step System -

1. Find It
2. Fund It
3. Finish It
4. Fill It
5. Future-Proof It

It enabled me to see the wood for the trees, and to be able to teach others about how to create a profitable HMO business. These steps are the backbone of what I teach now, and they will enable you to learn a simple method for finding and creating your first HMO, and creating that additional income stream each and every month.

If you're reading this and wondering exactly how to do it, then I want to give you some headline tools and tips in this chapter. [For more information, please look up my two books on investing in HMOs – '101 Essential Tips for Running a Professional HMO1' and 'Extraordinary Profits from Ordinary Properties' – both on Amazon].

Final tips for creating wealth through HMOs

1. Your mindset and belief system will shape you more than you realise – so spend time around people (and listen to podcasts, watch videos and read books) of people who you want to emulate. You'll find that their mindset was key to their success. Knowledge helps you learn but mindset makes you grow.

2. Set a goal. It could be a small goal to start with or a Big Hairy Audacious Goal! Whichever you choose, make sure you write out a manageable plan with actions and steps. If you need to tweak it once it's written that's fine. Goals without a plan are just daydreams and hopes.

3. Find an accountability partner who can share your journey with you. If you decide to follow my Five Step System to creating a profitable HMO portfolio, there will be lots to learn and do.

An accountability partner will keep you objective on your path, focused on your actions and mindful of your next steps so that you can implement your plan.

4. Finally, enjoy it! Have fun, and see this as a new adventure in your life. Be wise, be optimistic and take considered risks – go outside your comfort zone and very soon, you could have a house making you an extra £1000 per month income.

Wendy is the host of the HMO Success Podcast – a weekly show that discusses all things to do with HMOs. She is here to help you create a profitable HMO portfolio and her podcast contains a mixture of interviews, commentaries and discussions focused around the topic of Houses of Multiple Occupation. You can listen to her on Amazon, Spotify, Google and iTunes.

A Note from Kylie Anderson

"The number one reason most people don't get what they want is that they don't know what they want. Rich people are totally clear that they want wealth."

– T. Harv Eker

Thank you for purchasing a copy of this book, as you've probably now experienced through reading these chapters, Wealth isn't just about money, it's about so much more.

Yet money is an integral part, as it's a resource for you to help others, live the life you want and have more time freedom. It's time we stop avoiding it!

There are many ways to build your income and grow your long term wealth.

As women, a big part of our growth is through collaboration and helping others along the way. I therefore hope that this collaboration of incredible women sharing their wisdom and insights around their own journeys, has inspired you to broaden your knowledge, develop new skills and break out of your comfort zone to go for what you really want in your life.

If you'd love to connect with not only me but these amazing women experts too – join the Iconic Wealth for Women community – Go To – www.iconicwealthforwomen.com

"Wealth is largely the result of habit."

John Jacob Astor

Knowledge without action is just information.

It's the small step by step actions you can take to develop your long term wealth, creating a life you truly desire and helping others along the way!.

This could simply be...

- Not spending on that one takeaway a week or cancelling one monthly subscription and investing the money instead (remember you don't have to start with big money, it's the small compounding money that can make a big difference to your future – I personally started with a simple index tracker.)
- Developing a growth money mindset – journaling daily, working on limiting beliefs that hold you back – the first step to overcoming these is creating awareness around them.
- Learning something new that gives you the knowledge to grow your wealth.
- Making a new connection or creating a collaboration to work together and help each other.

Download your free **WEALTH AUDIT checklist here**: **www.iconicwealthforwomen.com/book-resources**

The first step is knowing your current position, this checklist will help you to understand your current financial situations so we have a great place to start from (no matter what stage of your journey you are on).

There are also some other fabulous resources to help you create an action plan for your wealth journey.

Whatever you are looking to achieve, you can create it!

Let's build and grow together.

I personally can't wait to hear about your journey, and would love to hear your updates in our community and remember if someone like me (or other ladies in this book) can create the life they truly desire, you can too.

"What's keeping you from being rich?
In most cases it's simply a lack of belief. In order to become rich, you must believe you can do it, and you must take the actions necessary to achieve your goal."
– Suze Orman

About Kylie Anderson, the Founder of Iconic Wealth for Women

Kylie Anderson is an Online Business Strategist & Award Winning Coach helping coaches & service based business owners turn their existing knowledge & skills into high ticket online programs so they can move from 1:1 to 1:many and have more recurring revenue and time freedom. With one simple shift in her business she added another £100k to her bottom line during the global pandemic in 2021.

With over 15 years of corporate sales and business experience, doing millions of dollars in deals, she has now gone on to build a multi six figure online coaching business giving her more time and freedom.

Her straight talking, no bull**** approach along with NLP Mastery helps her clients to cut through the fluff, change their beliefs, find out what works for them the most and get results! Implement Implement Implement.

Now the Founder of Iconic Wealth for Women – **OUR MISSION** is to help one million women create more Income, Impact and Influence – growing their wealth to grow their legacy!

An Aussie living in the UK for over 15 years who loves to travel (45 different places and counting), helping others create a ripple effect with their gifts and helping women create more wealth.

Connect with her via LinkedIN – www.linkedin.com/in/kylieandersoncq/

Or nosy at her website – https://kylieandersoncoaching.com/

And join the **ICONIC WEALTH FOR WOMEN COMMUNITY – Go To** – www.iconicwealthforwomen.com/

IN PARTNERSHIP WITH Elle Bright, creator of:

ELLEBRIGHT.COM

The **Revolutionary Method** that releases you from the Inner Conflict that causes Imposter Syndrome, Overwhelm, Burnout and the feeling of "Never Enough" so that you can Create the Income, Time Freedom and Joy you truly desire.

Hi, **I'm Elle Bright (Gok Wan MBE's tour photographer)** and I specialise in supporting Women Entrepreneurs to make the necessary pattern interrupt so that you can Leap into your **QUANTUM IDENTITY.**

Why is this "revolutionary"? Because action and physical proof are the highest form of communication. You will concretise your new patterns of emotion, thought and action that we defined through mindset and bodywork into YOUR REALITY with personalised challenges including a Confidence-Boosting Boudoir Photoshoot so that you can feel and experience your womanly power and break through your Imposter Syndrome and have beautiful Boudoir Photos of you as physical proof of your Quantum Identity Transformation.

Overcome Imposter Syndrome and make your Quantum Identity Leap to the Success you desire.

Get Your Free Assessment & Guide at:
https://ellebright.com/freeguide

Get our Special Offer for Iconic Wealth:
https://ellebright.com/iconicwealth

Join Our Community:
https://www.facebook.com/groups/brightwoman

IN PARTNERSHIP WITH Sarah Mapes, creator of:

"One in three women and one in five men will experience an osteoporotic fracture in their lifetime."

The cost of treating osteoporotic fractures is estimated to be between 5 trillion and 7 trillion dollars every year, not including the costs of disability and lost productivity. 25% of all post menopausal women will experience a vertebral fracture during their lifetime.

These statistics along with going through the repercussions of a fall with my own Grandma (my reason behind all that I do…) when she was diagnosed with osteoporosis after experiencing a hip fracture our world changed.

Hey **I'm Sarah Mapes, Bone Density specialist**, a 500 hour trained yoga teacher with 40 hours of training specific to yoga and osteoporosis through Yoga Alliance.

I'm also a certified Bone Fit Trainer with the Bone Health and Osteoporosis Foundation and also became a certified integrative nutrition health coach through IIN, The Institute for Integrative Nutrition.

I now help clients not only prevent deterioration in their bone density, but manage the symptoms of an Osteoporosis diagnosis too.

Manage and even prevent the loss of bone density in your future with our **8 Step Bone Builder System.**

**Free Guide –
"3 Things You Can Do NOW To Reduce Your Risk of
an Osteoporotic Bone Fracture."**

**https://about.bonebuildersystem.com/3-ways-to-reduce-osteo-
fractures**

Join our Bone Builders Community:
https://www.facebook.com/groups/bonebuilders

Ingram Content Group UK Ltd.
Milton Keynes UK
UKHW020855280423
420926UK00001B/1